# Ulster Cooking

# The best from the North Coast

*Including*
*Handy Hints for the kitchen and around the home*

# Contents

# Breakfasts

•••••••••••••••••••••••

# MUESLI

1¼ lb. coarse porridge oats
10 oz. wheatgerm
8 oz. brown sugar
8 oz. coconut
2 cups breakfast bran flakes
2 level teaspoons salt
2 rounded teaspoons cinnamon
2 rounded teaspoons mixed spice
1 cup cooking vegetable oil
2 cups milk
Add, after cooking the above.
8 oz. raisins or sultanas
4 oz. mixed chopped nuts
1 cup sunflower or sesame seeds

Mix all dry ingredients in a large bowl. Add oil and milk and stir until well coated. Bake, uncovered in two large roasting tins at gas mark 1, 275°F, 140°C for 45 minutes (Stir every 15 minutes). Add seeds, fruit and nuts. Store in airtight containers.


# ALL DAY BREAKFAST

4 sausages
2 slices black pudding
2 slices white pudding
4 rashers of bacon (rindless)
12 medium-size mushrooms
2 tomatoes (halved)
2 potato farls
2 eggs

Before cooking, keep the oven on at a low setting for keeping the food warm before serving. Prick the sausages a few times then gently fry or grill until well cooked through and evenly browned. Fry the black and white pudding then keep warm with the sausages. Fry the bacon. After draining off the fat, keep warm. Fry the mushrooms, the tomatoes and the potato farls, adding a knob of butter if there is not enough fat in the pan. Finally fry the eggs, spooning the fat over the yolks. Serve.


# FRENCH TOAST

Fingers of bread
seasoning
1 egg
marg.

Beat egg, season, dip bread fingers into egg. Fry in marg. until golden brown on both sides. Serve with bacon.

# HAM FRITTERS

25g marg.
seasoning
4 rashers ham
3 tablespoons milk
75g self-raising flour

Melt fat, chop ham, fry until crisp. Put ham, flour, seasoning and milk in a bowl and beat well. Drop in spoonfuls of the mixture into hot bacon fat, flatten. Fry till golden brown on both sides.

# SAUSAGE, BACON, MUSHROOM AND BEAN BRUNCH

1 small tin baked beans
4 sausages, cut into pieces
4 rashers streaky bacon, cut into pieces
1 onion, sliced
4 oz. mushrooms, sliced
4 eggs

4 tablespoons double cream

Fry bacon and sausages until cooked. Add onion and mushrooms. Stir in beans and heat gently. Season to taste. Spoon mixture into 4 ovenproof dishes. Crack an egg into each. Top with a spoonful of cream. Bake at gas mark 4, 350°F, 180°C for 10 mins until eggs are just set. Serve with triangles of fried bread or toast.

# PORRIDGE

1 litre of water
100 gm oatmeal
2 teaspoons salt

Boil water, add salt, sprinkle in oatmeal. Bring to the boil and stir frequently. Simmer for 20-30 mins.

# BACON, SAUSAGE AND APPLE

4 rashers of bacon
2 sausages
1 apple

Remove rind from bacon, prick sausages skin, core and slice apple. Cook sausages slowly for 4 mins, add bacon and cook until fat is clear and crisp. Remove from pan. Fry apple rings till soft. Serve with bacon and sausages.

# *Starters* ◆◆◆◆◆◆◆◆◆◆◆◆◆◆◆◆◆◆◆◆◆◆◆◆◆◆◆◆

# CREAMY VEGETABLE SOUP

1 oz. butter
4 oz. button mushrooms, sliced
2 onions, finely chopped
6 oz. carrots
1 tablespoon chopped parsley
2 celery stalks, sliced
850ml chicken stock
3 tablespoons cornflour
1 small green pepper
300ml milk
3 tablespoons single cream
salt and pepper
bread croutons, to garnish (optional)

Melt the butter in a large saucepan, add the onions and fry gently for 5 mins. Add carrots and celery, cook for 2-3 mins, stirring occasionally. Add the chicken stock, bring to the boil, then lower the heat, cover and simmer gently for 30 mins. Add the green pepper, mushrooms and parsley. Cook for 15-20 mins. In a bowl, blend cornflour with a little of the milk to form a paste. Stir the remaining milk into the pan, then add the cornflour paste. Bring to the boil and simmer for 1 minute, stirring constantly. Remove from heat and stir in cream, then reheat gently. Season to taste.

# THICK TOMATO SOUP

3 potatoes, peeled and cubed
539g can of tomatoes
2 carrots, cubed
1 large onion, finely chopped
1 garlic cove, crushed
1 teaspoon dried basil or oregano
2 tablespoons vegetable oil
1 teaspoon castor sugar
300ml hot vegetable or chicken stock
salt and pepper

Gently fry the potatoes, carrots, onion and garlic in the oil for 5 mins. Add the tomatoes with their juice and half the stock, stirring to break up the tomatoes. Bring to the boil. Add the basil or oregano and sugar and season with salt and pepper. Lower the heat and simmer very gently, covered, for about 20 minutes, until the vegetables are tender. Roughly purée the soup in a blender for a few seconds. Return to the saucepan and add enough stock to give the required consistency; the soup should be quite thick. Heat through and adjust the seasoning. Serve at once.

# LETTUCE SOUP

1 large lettuce
1 medium onion
1 medium potato
2 oz. butter
1 stock cube
¼ pint milk
salt and pepper
chopped parsley

Melt butter in saucepan. Wash and shred lettuce, dice potato, slice onion. Put vegetables into melted butter and sauté for 15 minutes. Add stock cube and milk. Bring to boil and simmer 10 – 15 minutes. Liquidize when cool. Reheat and serve garnished with chopped parsley.


# PARSNIP & POTATO SOUP

1 oz. butter
2 onions, chopped
12 oz. parsnips, peeled and chopped
1 potato, peeled and chopped
1 small teaspoon curry powder
1¼ pint chicken stock
salt and pepper
2 tablespoons chopped parsley

Melt butter in a large saucepan. Gently cook onions, parsnips and potato for about 5 minutes. Add curry powder, stock and seasoning, bring to the boil. Reduce the heat, cover and simmer for 20 minutes until vegetables are cooked. Puree soup in blender or food processor. Return to saucepan and reheat. Stir in parsley and serve.


# BROCCOLI SOUP

1 head of Broccoli,
broken into florets and washed
1 oz. butter
1 large potato, peeled and sliced
1 large onion, peeled and sliced
1½ pints of stock
salt and pepper

Melt butter in a large saucepan. Add vegetables. Stir to prevent burning. Add stock, salt and pepper. Bring to boil and cook until vegetables are tender. Blend in a food processor. If the soup is too thick add some milk. Reheat, garnish with chopped parsley, and serve.

# NUTTY PEACHES (Serves 2)

4 lettuce leaves
4 peach halves
3 oz. sweetcorn
1 oz. salted peanuts
4 oz. cheddar cheese, grated
1-2 tablespoons double cream
lightly whipped
1-2 tablespoons salad cream
4 slices cucumber

Drain peaches and place on lettuce leaves. Mix sweetcorn, nuts, cheese, and bind together with cream and salad cream. Season. Pile mixture on top of each peach half, and garnish with cucumber slices.


# STUFFED PEARS

Lettuce leaves
6 pear halves, drained
½ cup grated raw carrot
1 tablespoon raisins
1 tablespoon chopped walnuts
mayonnaise
tomato to garnish

Arrange pear halves on lettuce leaves. Combine carrot, raisins and nuts. Moisten with mayonnaise. Pile this mixture on to the pear halves. Garnish with sliced tomatoes.


# PRAWN COCKTAIL

4 oz. prawns
4 drops tobasco
2 tablespoons tomato ketchup
1 tablespoon sweet sherry
3 tablespoons mayonnaise
2 tablespoons fresh cream

Stir all ingredients into a bowl and place in fridge for at least 1 hour before serving. Serve all in a tall glass on a bed of shredded lettuce with a slice of lemon on the rim and the prawns and sauce sprinkled with a little cayenne pepper.

# MINTED MELON

2 small melons
4 oz. seedless green grapes
2 tablespoons colmans
sweet mint jelly
2 kiwi fruit peeled and sliced
1 large pear or green apple, sliced
1 small banana, sliced

Cut melons in half in a zigzag pattern, discard seeds. Remove melon flesh with melon baller. Place melon balls and grapes into a glass bowl with mint jelly and chill overnight. Add remaining fruit about 1 hour before serving. Serve inside melon shells.

# EGG MAYONNAISE

4 large eggs
1 lettuce
4-6 tablespoons mayonnaise
paprika
cress

Hard boil the eggs. Wash and dry the lettuce and arrange on individual plates. Shell and halve the eggs and place on the lettuce. Spoon the mayonnaise over the eggs. Sprinkle with paprika. Decorate with cress.

# DRESSED CRAB

2 medium sized crabs
2 eggs
1 teaspoon mustard
1 teaspoon chives, chopped
1 teaspoon parsley, chopped

Place crabs in a saucepan of salted water, bring to the boil and then simmer gently for 30 mins. Drain and allow the crabs to cool. Remove the claws and undershells. Take out the brown creamy part and put it aside in a bowl. Remove all the meat from the claws, by cracking them open. Mix together the white meat and blend the mustard and salt and pepper with the brown creamy part. Arrange the white and brown mixtures side by side in the shells. Hard boil the eggs then chop with the chives and parsley and sprinkle on top of the crab mixture. Serve with a green salad.

# PRAWNS WITH GARLIC AND FRESH HERBS

2lb Dublin Bay prawns
in their shells
2 cloves of garlic, crushed
8 oz. butter
1 tablespoon parsley, chopped
1 tablespoon dill, chopped
juice of lemon
salt and pepper

Boil a large pan of salted water. Add the prawns. Remove them when they float in the water. Shell the prawns when cool. Melt the butter in a pan on a low setting and add the garlic, parsley, dill and lemon juice. Add salt and pepper to taste. Add the prawns and reheat them, still on a low setting, so that they do not become tough. Serve with fresh brown crusty bread and a green salad.

# FRUIT COCKTAIL

1 apple
1 pear
1 orange
50g grapes
50g pineapple
½ grapefruit
Syrup
125ml pineapple juice and water
juice of ½ lemon
sugar to taste

Add lemon juice to the liquid. Prepare fruit and cut up roughly. Liquidise fruit with the liquid, chill and serve in glasses with a cherry on top.

# LENTIL & BACON BROTH

2 tablespoons oil
3 oz. smoked bacon, rinded and chopped
8 oz. onions, chopped
8 oz. carrots, peeled and chopped
10 oz. lentils, trimmed and chopped
6 oz. celery scrubbed, trimmed and chopped
1½ pts chicken stock
pinch of nutmeg
1 bay leaf
½ teaspoon dried thyme
salt and freshly ground black pepper

Put oil in saucepan, add the bacon, onion, carrot and celery, fry for 5 minutes stirring occasionally. Add the lentils and stir in the stock, nutmeg bay leaf, thyme and seasoning. Bring to the boil, then cover the pan and simmer for 45 minutes until the lentils are soft. Remove the bay leaf and puree the soup in a blender. Taste and adjust the seasoning. Suitable for freezing.
Serves 8 – 10.

14

# Fish Dishes

# CREAMY COD BAKE

700g cod fillet,
skinned and cut into 4 cm cubes
1 onion, chopped
30g marg.
4 tablespoons dry white wine
black pepper
700g potatoes
255g smoked bacon rashers, halved
salt
150ml single cream
2 tablespoons grated Parmesan cheese
paprika

Cooking temperature – gas mark 5, 375°F, 190°C
Put the fish cubes in a shallow dish and sprinkle over the onion. Spoon over the wine and turn the fish carefully to coat. Cover and leave to marinate for 2 hours, turning the fish very carefully from time to time. Put the potatoes in a large saucepan of salted water, bring to the boil, cover and boil gently for about 15 mins until just tender, but not soft. Drain well and leave to cool slightly. Brush a shallow ovenproof casserole with some of the melted fat. Cut the potatoes into 5mm slices and arrange them in a single layer in the base of the casserole. Brush the potatoes with remaining fat and season. Using a slotted spoon, remove the fish and onion from the marinade and arrange the fish and chopped onion on top of the potatoes. Arrange the bacon on top of the fish. Bake for 15 mins and then lower the heat to gas mark 4, 350°F, 180°C. Pour the cream over the top of the casserole, sprinkle with the Parmesan cheese and season the top with a little paprika. Return the casserole to the oven for a further 15-20 mins, until the topping is golden. Serve hot, straight from the casserole.

# SALMON PIE

1 medium tin red salmon
8 oz. mashed potatoes
¼ pint milk
1 oz. butter
2 eggs, separated
salt and pepper
Squeeze lemon juice
chopped parsley

Bring milk and butter to boil and beat in the potatoes. Gently add flaked salmon, egg yolks, parsley, and squeeze lemon juice. Fold in well-beaten egg whites. Put into an ovenproof dish and bake for 30 minutes at gas mark 4, 350°F, 180°C. Serve with peas and sweetcorn.

# HADDOCK & BROCCOLI BAKE

12 oz. smoked haddock
12 fl ozs. milk
1 oz. butter
1 oz. plain flour
salt and pepper
4 oz. mature cheddar cheese, grated
8 oz. broccoli florets (cooked)
3 tomatoes
1 lbs. potatoes, cooked and sliced.

Poach fish in the milk. Strain and reserve the liquid. Flake fish and discard any bones and skin. Melt butter and stir in flour. Gradually stir in the fish cooking liquid and bring to the boil. Simmer until thickened, season and add 2 oz. of grated cheese and the fish. Place broccoli in an ovenproof dish and top with the fish mixture. Cover with tomato slices and the potato slices. Sprinkle with remaining 2 oz. grated cheese. Bake at gas mark 6, 400°F, 200°C for 30 minutes until golden brown. Sprinkle with chopped parsley and serve.

# KEDGEREE

500g fish
(salmon, haddock or smoked)
curry powder
250g patma rice
2 hard boiled eggs
50g marg.
lemon and parsley, for garnish
salt

Wash and dry fish, poach or steam till tender. Drain and flake, removing bones and skin. Wash rice and place in boiling water and salt. Boil for 10-12 mins till cooked. Drain and pour boiling water through and drain again. Melt marg. in a pan and re-heat rice and haddock by tossing in marg. Season and add curry powder to taste. Chop one egg and add to fish, slice second egg for garnish. Serve on an oval dish, garnish with egg, lemon and parsley. This dish may be served hot or cold.

# FISH AND TOMATO CASSEROLE

½ lb fish
parsley, finely chopped
few tomatoes, sliced
1 onion, chopped finely
2 oz. grated cheese
2 oz. breadcrumbs

Put fish into casserole dish. Sprinkle with salt and pepper. Place tomatoes, onion, and parsley into a pan and simmer for 10-15 mins. Add to fish once simmered. Mix cheese and breadcrumbs and sprinkle on top. Decorate top with parsley. Cook at gas mark 4, 350°F, 180°C for 30 mins.

 *Handy Hints* *When you move house leave the new residents some self-addressed sticky labels (new address). Post can be forwarded without any bother.*

# TUNA FISH CURRY

300ml milk
55g desiccated coconut
1 tablespoon vegetable oil
1 onion, sliced
1 green pepper, seeded and sliced
2 cloves garlic, crushed
2 teaspoons ground cardamom
2 teaspoons ground ginger
1 teaspoon ground turmeric
150ml water
½ - ¼ teaspoon chilli powder
2 * 200g tins of tuna
juice of 1 lemon
salt and black pepper
2 hard-boiled eggs, sliced
coriander leaves, to garnish

Put the milk and coconut into a saucepan and heat slowly just to simmering point. Remove from the heat, cover and leave for 20 mins. Strain milk with the back of a wooden spoon. Reserve the milk and discard the coconut. Heat the oil in a large saucepan, add onion and green pepper and fry gently for 5 mins. Add garlic and spices. Cook for 1-2 mins. Combine the coconut milk with the water and gradually stir into the pan. Bring slowly to the boil, then lover heat and simmer, uncovered, for 5 mins, stirring occasionally. Stir in tuna and lemon juice, and season. Cover and simmer very gently for 10-15 mins. Transfer to a warmed serving dish, garnish and serve.

# MUSSELS IN A CREAMY SAUCE

3 dozen mussels in their shells, well scrubbed, beards removed
4 oz. chopped leeks
2 oz. chopped celery
2 oz. chopped onions
1 pint white wine or dry cider
300ml double cream
2 oz. butter
chopped parsley
salt, pepper and nutmeg

Scrub the mussels thoroughly; discard any that are open. Bring the vegetables and wine or cider to the boil in a large pan and then drop in the mussels. Cook till they begin to open, then remove from the heat and cover for 10 mins, shaking the pan occasionally until most have opened. Discard any that remain closed. Remove the mussels. Retain the stock, strain through a fine sieve and return it to the pan. Set the mussels aside. Taste the stock. Add the cream, butter, parsley and season with salt, pepper and nutmeg. Add the mussels in half-shells and heat them through.

 *H*andy *H*ints *When getting to the end of a mustard jar, fill with water and shake well. Add the liquid to gravy for extra bite.*

# CREAM OF SALMON SOUP

1 lb whiting, skinned, boned and cut into 1" cube
8 oz. smoked salmon pieces
1 onion, finely chopped
1 small potato, chopped
1 small carrot grated
2 oz. butter
6 dessertspoons plain flour
½ pt water
½ pt milk
¼ pt whipping cream
pepper
garnish, chopped parsley

Combine fish, salmon, onion, carrot, potato. Place in a deep bowl, cover with water and cook on high for 5 mins. Place in a blender, add milk and puree until smooth. Rinse out the bowl and melt for 1 min on high. Stir in the flour and gradually pour in the fish and milk mixture. Heat for 5 mins on high. Add pepper and cream and reheat for 5 min on high. Sprinkle with chopped parsley and serve.

# FISHERMAN'S PIE

2 lb potatoes, peeled, boiled and sliced thickly
1 oz. butter
1 oz. flour
4 fl ozs. dry white wine
½ pt milk
4 tablespoons chopped parsley
salt and black pepper
1½ lb whiting, poached and flaked
2 hard-boiled eggs

Cooking Temperature gas mark 6, 400°F, 200°C
Boil potatoes, cool and slice. Melt butter in saucepan and stir in the flour. Remove from heat and whisk in the wine. Return to heat and gradually add milk. Whisk until the sauce thickens. Add chopped parsley. Season to taste. Gently add the flaked fish and eggs. Place in an ovenproof dish. Top with potato slices. Bake for 20-25 mins until golden and bubbling. Serve with peas.

 *Handy Hints* *To save a cake that has sunk in the middle, cut out the centre and then fill with fruit and whipped cream.*

*Add a teaspoon of lemon juice when boiling cabbage to reduce smells.*

*A tablespoon of milk added to cauliflower will help keep it white.*

*Use crushed cornflakes for a crispier coating for fish or scotch eggs.*

# SAVOURY HADDOCK FLAN

### Cheese Pastry
30oz butter
30oz cheddar cheese, grated
5oz plain flour
### Filling
1lb smoked haddock (poached and flaked)
### Parsley Sauce
1oz butter
1oz plain flour
½ pint milk
1 tbsp parsley, chopped
### Topping
1½ lb potatoes (peeled, boiled, mashed)
1 tbsp milk
spring onions cut up

### Pastry
Cream butter and cheese together. Gradually work in the flour to form a smooth dough. Refrigerate for 30 mins. Roll out to line a 8" flan ring. Bake at gas mark 6, 400°F, 200°C for 20 mins. Cool and transfer to an ovenproof dish.
### Parsley Sauce
Melt butter, stir in flour and cook for 1 min. Gradually add milk, whisking all the time. Bring to the boil and boil for 1 further min. Add parsley. Fold in fish and pour into flan case.
### Topping
Mash potatoes, add butter, milk and chopped spring onions. Pile on top of fish mixture, or pipe in rosettes over fish. Bake for 30 mins at gas mark 5, 375°F, 190°C. Serve hot with a green salad.

# SALMON AND TUNA LOAF

½ oz. melted butter
7½ oz. can salmon, drained and mashed
7 oz. can tuna, drained and mashed
2 oz. brown breadcrumbs
4 oz. onion grated
1½ oz. walnuts, finely chopped
salt and black pepper
1 teaspoon dry mustard
2 eggs, beaten
2 teaspoons dried mixed herbs
1 teaspoon Worcester sauce
7 oz. can tomatoes, drained and chopped

Cooking Temperature - gas mark 5, 375°F, 190°C
Line a 1lb loaf tin with foil and brush with melted butter. Combine fish with all remaining ingredients. Mix thoroughly and spoon into loaf tin. Smooth the top and cook until firm (approx. 50-55 mins). Leave until lukewarm before turning out of tin. Slice when cold. Serve as a starter on lettuce leaves or as a main course with salad.

# Main Meals & Savouries

# SWEET & SOUR PORK

1lb Pork pieces
4 tablespoons vinegar
1 lge onion
salt & pepper
¼ lb mushrooms
2 dessertspoons cornflour
1 tablespoon soy sauce
small tin pineapple
3 tablespoons soft brown sugar

Fry pork, onions and mushrooms. Combine pineapple juice and water to make half a pint. Add sugar, soy sauce and vinegar. Blend in cornflour and bring to the boil. Pour over pork. Cook at gas mark 4, 350°F, 180°C for 1 hour or 1 and a half hours.

# SHEPHERD'S PIE

2lb potatoes
8 fl oz. strong beef stock
1 tablespoons vegetable oil
1 tablespoon chopped fresh parsley
1 onion, chopped
salt and pepper
1 clove garlic, crushed
3 tablespoons milk
1lb lean minced beef
knob of butter
1 red pepper, seeded
3 oz. grated cheddar cheese
1 tablespoon plain flour

Cooking Temperature – gas mark 6, 400°F, 200°C
Cut potatoes into even-sized pieces. Put in a pan of lightly salted boiling water and cook until tender. Drain. Meanwhile, heat oil in a large frying pan and fry onions for 3-4 mins. Add garlic, mince and red pepper and cook, stirring, for 4-5 mins. Stir in the flour then add the stock and bring to the boil, stirring continuously. Add parsley and seasoning. Mash potatoes and mix with milk and butter. Season. Spoon mince into an ovenproof dish, top with potato, sprinkle with cheese and bake for 30 mins.

# CHILLI CON CARNE

1 tablespoon vegetable oil
3 tablespoons tomato purée
2 onions, chopped
2 * 400g can tomatoes
1 clove garlic, crushed
150ml strong beef stock
1lb lean minced beef
2 * 450g can red kidney beans
salt and pepper
parsley sprigs to garnish
1-2 teaspoons hot chilli powder OR 1-2 chilli peppers

Heat oil in a large saucepan, add onion and garlic and fry until soft. Add mince and fry until browned. Add seasoning and chilli powder or chillies. Stir in tomato purée, tomatoes and stock. Bring to the boil, cover and simmer for 45 mins. Add kidney beans, cover and simmer for 15 mins. Serve chilli on a bed of rice, garnished with parsley.

# LASAGNE

2 tablespoons vegetable oil
400g can tomatoes
2 onions, chopped
2 tablespoons tomato purée
1 clove garlic, crushed
300ml beef stock
1 carrot, chopped
salt and pepper
1lb lean minced beef
12 sheets oven ready lasagne
50g Parmesan cheese, grated
**Cheese Sauce**
75g butter
pinch grated nutmeg
75g plain flour
50g cheddar cheese, grated
800ml milk

Cooking temperature – gas mark 4, 350°F, 180°C
Grease a 3 litre ovenproof dish. Heat oil in a large pan and fry onions, garlic and carrot for 4-5 mins. Add mince and fry for 3-4 mins until brown. Stir in tomatoes, tomato purée, stock and seasoning. Simmer, covered, for 30 mins. Melt butter, add flour and stir for 1 min. Remove from heat and gradually add milk. Bring to the boil, stirring until thick. Season and add cheddar cheese. Preheat oven. Put 4 sheets of lasagne in dish, cover with half meat sauce then third cheese sauce. Repeat layers, finishing with lasagne, cheese sauce and Parmesan. Bake for 45 mins.

# BACON AND EGG PIE

6 oz. plain flour
1 beaten egg and water to mix
3 oz. marg.
pinch salt
**Filling**
⅓ lb streaky bacon (chopped)
3 beaten eggs
1 medium onion (chopped)
¼ pint milk
3 oz. grated cheese

Cooking temperature – gas mark 4, 350°F, 180°C
Rub marg. into flour and salt. Blend together with the beaten egg and water mix to make pastry. Roll out and put into a fluted flat dish. Fry chopped bacon and onion. Beat eggs into milk. Add cooked bacon and onion. Pour into uncooked pastry case. Cook for approx. 35 mins.

*H**andy** H**ints*** *Fruitcakes will keep longer if an apple is put in the airtight tin with the cakes.*

*When ironing place the largest flat item (tablecloth) on the ironing board before pressing smaller items over it. The tablecloth will then need less ironing.*

# VEGETABLE FRIED RICE

9 oz. long grain rice
1 large onion, chopped
9 oz. carrots, diced
1 clove garlic, crushed
1 parsnip, diced
2 oz. button mushrooms
1 small turnip, diced
2 large tomatoes, skinned and sliced
2 tablespoons vegetable oil
2 oz. frozen peas
black pepper
2 eggs lightly beaten
1 tablespoon chopped fresh parsley
grated Parmesan cheese, to serve

Bring a large saucepan of salted water to the boil, add the rice and cover. Lower the heat and simmer for 10 minutes, or until the rice is just tender. Meanwhile, bring another pan of salted water to the boil. Add the carrots, parsnip and turnip and cover. Lower the heat and cook for about 8-10mins, or until all the vegetables are barely tender. Drain the cooked root vegetables and reserve. Drain the rice in a colander and rinse well under hot running water to separate the grains. Drain again. Heat the oil in a large non-stick saucepan, add the onion and garlic and fry gently for 5 mins until soft and lightly coloured. Add the drained root vegetables to the pan, together with the mushrooms, tomatoes, peas and rice. Stir well and season to taste with salt and plenty of pepper. Cover the pan and cook over very low heat for 10 mins. Stir in the eggs and gently turn the mixture so that the egg cooks. Remove from the heat and turn into a warmed serving dish. Garnish with the parsley and serve at once with the Parmesan cheese.

# PORK ESCALOPES WITH PLUMS

9 oz. red plums
1 teaspoon cinnamon
2 tablespoons vegetable oil
½ teaspoon ground coriander
1 onion, finely chopped
salt and pepper
150ml cider or dry white wine
8 pork escalopes, each weighing 50g

Remove the stones from the plums. To make the sauce, heat half the oil in a pan, add the onion and fry gently for 10 mins until softened. Pour in the cider and bring to the boil. Add the spices and salt and pepper to taste. Stir well, then lower the heat, cover and cook the sauce gently for 5 mins. Add the plums to the sauce, cover and simmer very gently for a further 10-15 mins. Taste and adjust the seasoning. Meanwhile, divide the remaining oil between 2 large frying pans and heat gently. Add the pork escalopes and cook over high heat for 3 minutes on each side until browned. To serve arrange the escalopes on warmed serving dish and spoon over the sauce. Serve at once.

24

# PARCELLED PORK CHOPS WITH SAGE

1 tablespoon vegetable oil
4 pork loin chops,
trimmed of excess fat
4 oz. mushrooms, thinly sliced
4-8 spring onions, finely chopped
2 courgettes, thinly sliced
salt and pepper
2 teaspoons dried sage

Cooking Temperature – gas mark 5, 375°F, 190°C

Heat the oil in a frying-pan, add the chops and brown on both sides over brisk heat. Remove from the pan and drain on absorbent paper. Mix together the courgettes, mushrooms and spring onions. Cut out 4 squares of foil each large enough to enclose a chop. Divide the mixed vegetables into 8 portions. Place a portion on each square of foil, and place the chops on top of the vegetables. Season with salt and pepper and sprinkle with the sage. Top with the remaining mixed vegetables. Fold the foil over the chops and vegetables to make neat parcels and place on a baking sheet. Cook in the oven for 45 mins or until the chops are cooked through. Serve the chops at once.

# CHICKEN AND CELERY PINWHEELS

1 pkt. packet of puff pastry
6 oz. cooked chopped chicken
2 sticks of celery
3 oz. grated cheddar cheese
2 tablespoons mayonnaise
2 tablespoons yoghurt
seasoning

Roll pastry to form a large rectangle. Mix the finely chopped chicken, cheese, mayonnaise and yoghurt. Spread the chicken mix on top of the rolled pastry and roll swiss roll style. Cut slices across the roll approx. $\sum$ - $\Omega$ inch in thickness. Lay on a baking sheet, brush with beaten egg and bake for 20 mins at gas mark 6, 400°F, 200°C.

# TOMATO SALAD

4-6 ripe tomatoes
salt and pepper
2 tablespoons olive oil
2 tablespoons finely chopped parsley
2 teaspoons wine vinegar
1-2 garlic cloves, finely chopped

Wipe the tomatoes and cut them across into even slices. Arrange them in a serving dish. Mix together the olive oil, wine vinegar and salt and pepper to taste. Pour this dressing over the tomatoes. Sprinkle the salad with finely chopped parsley and garlic to taste.

# APPLE GLAZED CARROTS

1lb carrots
2 dessert apples
salt
1-2 tablespoons chopped mint
or parsley
1 teaspoon sugar
black pepper
15g butter
squeeze lemon juice
2 onions, halved and thinly sliced

Peel or scrape the carrots, then halve them and cut the halves lengthways into sticks. Put the carrot sticks in a pan of cold, lightly salted water and add the sugar. Boil the carrot sticks for 5-7 minutes, until almost tender but still slightly crisp. Meanwhile, melt the butter in a saucepan and fry the onions gently for 5 mins until soft. Drain the carrots, reserving 4 tablespoons of the cooking liquid. Peel, core and slice the apples. Add the drained carrots to the onions with the apples, the reserved cooking liquid, mint or parsley and salt and pepper to taste. Stir in lemon juice, if liked. Transfer to a warmed serving dish and serve.

# BROWN RICE RISOTTO

1 tablespoon vegetable oil
255g brown rice
1 onion, chopped
1pt vegetable stock
1 small green pepper, chopped
4 tomatoes, blanched, skinned and chopped
1 small red pepper, chopped
400g can red kidney beans
1 teaspoon mild chilli powder
salt and pepper

Heat the oil in a heavy-based saucepan and fry the onion gently for about 5 mins, until soft. Add the peppers and cook for 2-3 mins. Add the chilli powder and stir for 1 min, then add the rice and stir until the grains are shiny and coated with oil. Add half the stock, stir once and bring to the boil, then lower the heat and cook very gently until the liquid has been absorbed. Add half the remaining stock and cook until this has been absorbed too. Test the rice and if it is not tender add more stock and continue cooking. When the rice is cooked, add the tomatoes and kidney beans. Heat through for 2-3 mins, stirring gently. Season to taste with salt and pepper. Serve at once.

 *Handy Hints* *If your hair is suffering from the effects of hard water, add one tablespoon of bicarbonate of soda to the washing and rinsing water.*

*If a fat fire starts in a frying pan, use baking soda to smother the flames, not water.*

# VEGETABLE AND PASTA STIR-FRY

1lb wholewheat pasta shells
3 oz. green beans
1 oz. butter
half red and half green pepper
1 large onion, sliced
2 tablespoons soy sauce
3 celery stalks, cut into strips
salt and pepper
2 large carrots, cut into strips

Cook the pasta in plenty of boiling salted water for about 10 mins until tender. Drain and rinse under cold running water. Drain again. Melt the butter in a non-stick frying pan and add all the vegetables. Fry them gently for 10 mins, stirring frequently, until tender. Add the cooked pasta and soy sauce and cook for 2 minutes more, stirring to heat the pasta through. Season lightly with salt and pepper and serve.

# SAUSAGE AND BACON PIE

6 oz. butter / marg.
2-3 fl oz. water
12 oz. plain flour
beaten egg to glaze
Filling
12 oz. cocktail sausages
1 stick celery, finely chopped
1 tablespoon vegetable oil
1 oz. plain flour
1 oz. butter
8 fl oz. milk
2 onions, chopped
3 oz. cheddar cheese, grated
8 oz. bacon rashers, chopped
salt and pepper
2 tablespoons chopped parsley

Cooking Temperature – gas mark 6, 400°F, 200°C
Rub fat and flour together until mixture resembles fine breadcrumbs. Add sufficient cold water to form a firm dough. Cover and chill for 30 mins. Meanwhile, heat oil and fry sausages for 10 mins. Remove from pan and cool. Melt butter in pan, add onions, bacon and celery and sauté for 5-6 mins. Stir in flour and cook for 1 min. Remove from heat and gradually add milk. Return to heat and stir until sauce thickens and boils. Add cheese, sausages, parsley and seasoning, cover and leave to cool. Grease a 24cm flan tin. Roll out half pastry and line tin. Add filling. Roll out remaining pastry and cover pie. Decorate with pastry trimmings and make 3 vent holes in top. Brush with beaten egg and bake for 30-35 mins, until golden.

# LONG PASTA WITH GARLIC AND OIL

12 oz. linguine, spaghetti or vermicelli
salt
4 fl ozs. olive oil
3 tablespoons chopped parsley
3 garlic cloves, finely chopped
1 dry chilli, crushed

Put the pasta in a large pan of boiling salted water. When ready drain. Meanwhile, heat the oil in a large frying pan over medium heat, add the garlic, parsley and chilli and cook for 2 mins, stirring constantly. Add the pasta to the frying pan and cook it over medium low heat for 12 mins, stirring continually. Serve at once.

# BEEF OLIVES

5 slices of thin sirloin beef stuffed with bread stuffing, rolled and secured
2 onions
2 teaspoons thyme
Beef stock (enough to cover meat)
1 tablespoon tomato ketchup
2 teaspoons mustard
Cornflour

Cooking Temperature – gas mark 2, 300°F, 150°C
Heat oil in frying pan and fry olives until brown. Remove from pan and place in an ovenproof dish. Fry onion and thyme until brown. Add stock, seasoning, tomato ketchup and mustard. Bring to the boil and pour over the olives. Cover and cook for 45 minutes. Thicken the gravy with cornflour and serve along with vegetables and potatoes.

# CHICKEN STROGANOFF

2 tablespoons sunflower oil
25g butter
2 rashers of back bacon, chopped
2 medium onions thinly sliced
2 cloves garlic crushed
4 chicken fillets finely sliced
2 tablespoons plain flour
Salt
Freshly ground black pepper
250 g mushroom quartered
¼ pt chicken stock
150 ml carton soured cream
125 ml carton double cream

In a large heavy based saucepan heat the oil and butter together. Add the bacon, onions and garlic to the pan and sauté gently for 2-3 minutes. Add the mushrooms, sauté for a further minute. Place the flour in a bowl and add salt and pepper to season, add the chicken and toss well to coat completely with the seasoned flour. Add the chicken and any excess flour to the pan. Sauté gently for 3-4 minutes, taking care that the chicken does not burn. Add the stock, cover and simmer gently for 15 minutes. Just before serving remove the pan from the heat and stir in the soured then the double cream. Season to taste with some freshly ground black pepper. Serve with plain boiled rice or pasta.

# TASTY SNACKS

One slice of buttered bread for each person
1 slice of cheese
1 slice of ham, or cooked bacon
tomato slices
salt and pepper
chopped spring onion
OR
1 slice of ham
1 pineapple ring
1 slice of cheese
tomato slices

Place under the hot grill until cheese is soft.


Place under hot grill until cheese melts. Garnish with chopped parsley.

28

# CHICKEN WITH MUSHROOM AND GARLIC SAUCE (Serves 2)

2 chicken breasts
1 oz. butter
1 oz. garlic butter
4 oz. mushrooms, wiped and sliced
½ oz. Plain flour
¼ pint milk
6 tablespoons single cream

Heat butter in a pan and fry chicken breasts until golden brown on both sides. Cover pan, reduce the heat and continue cooking slowly for 20 minutes until the chicken is thoroughly cooked. In another pan heat the garlic butter, add the sliced mushrooms and cook gently. Sprinkle in the flour and cook for 1 minute. Gradually add the milk, stirring all the time until the sauce is smooth. Simmer for a further 2 minutes. Stir in the cream and gently heat through, but not boiled. Place cooked chicken on warmed serving plates, pour sauce over. Serve with green tagliatelle or rice. Garnish with chopped chives or parsley.

# CHICKEN HOTPOT

2 tablespoons sunflower oil
4 chicken drumsticks
4 chicken thigh portions
1 teaspoon chilli powder
2 oz. red lentils
½ pint chicken stock
14 oz. can chopped tomatoes
1 green pepper, deseeded and sliced
8 oz. can pineapple pieces
4 oz. can sweetcorn, drained
salt and pepper

Heat oil in a large pan and fry chicken pieces until browned on all sides. Sprinkle chilli powder over and cook for one minute. Add lentils, stock and chopped tomatoes. Bring to the boil, cover and simmer for 20 minutes. Add pepper slices, pineapple and sweetcorn, season. Cook uncovered for a further 20 minutes. Serve with boiled rice.

 *Handy Hints* *The PC mouse will run more smoothly if the ball underneath and the mouse mat is rubbed with a sheet of fabric conditioner.*

*Starching tights means they will not snag so easily.*

*Royal standing H.M. The Queen who is used to standing for long periods at royal events recommends that anyone who has to stand for prolonged periods should stand with both feet closer together as it is much easier.*

# CRUNCHY CHICKEN PIE

8 oz. cooked chicken
1 large leek
½ yellow pepper
1 oz. butter
1 oz. flour
½ pt. milk
salt and pepper
4 potatoes peeled and sliced
2 oz. cheddar cheese (grated)

Cook potatoes in salted water until just tender. Melt butter in a pan and fry the leeks. Add chopped pepper. Stir in flour and seasoning and cook for 1 minute. Blend in the milk and cook until the sauce thickens. Gently add the cooked chicken. Turn into an ovenproof casserole dish. Arrange the sliced potatoes on top. Sprinkle with grated cheese. Cook at gas mark 4, 350°F, 180°C for 20 – 30 minutes.

# HOT CHICKEN SALAD *(Good for using left over Chicken)*

Into a casserole dish put:
Layer of cooked chicken
Layer of chopped celery
1 chopped and deseeded green pepper
1 chopped onion
Mix together and pour over chicken:
½ cup of mayonnaise
1 tin Campbell's Condensed Chicken Soup
Juice of ½ a lemon
salt and pepper

Top with grated cheese and crushed Cheese & Onion Potato Crisps.
Bake at gas mark 4, 350°F, 180°C for 20 – 30 minutes.

# CRUNCHY CREAMED MUSHROOMS

12 oz. button mushrooms
2 oz. butter
½ oz. flour
¼ pint double cream
Seasoning
1 clove garlic (optional)

**Topping**
2 oz. cheddar cheese, grated
1 oz. breadcrumbs
1 oz. butter

Wipe mushrooms, trim stalks. Melt butter in pan, add mushrooms and garlic. Cook gently for a few minutes. Add flour to absorb excess moisture then add cream. Stirring all the time. Season, divide between 4 serving dishes.

**Topping**
Melt butter, add breadcrumbs and cheese. Sprinkle over mixture in serving dishes. Grill until crisp.

# NEW YORK CAESAR SALAD

4 thick slices white bread,
crusts removed
6 tablespoons olive oil
2 cos lettuce hearts
2 oz. parmesan cheese
Dressing
2 teaspoons capers (optional)
1 clove garlic
3 tablespoons olive oil
juice of 1 lemon
6 tablespoons single cream
¼ teaspoon mustard
salt and black pepper

Cut the bread into 1cm cubes. Heat the oil in a frying pan. Fry the bread cubes for 8 mins, turning occasionally, until golden. Tear the lettuce leaves and put in a salad bowl. Shave half the cheese into curls and grate the rest. Add the curls to the bowl with the croutons. For the dressing, chop the capers, if using, and peel and chop the garlic. Set the pan over a medium heat and add the olive oil, capers, lemon, garlic, cream, mustard and grated parmesan. Heat, whisking all the time, until well blended. Season to taste and pour over the salad. Toss and serve.
For a heartier dish, fry strips of chicken breast and add to the salad along with the croutons.

# CRISPY HERBED POTATOES

1¾ lbs potatoes
2 red onions
6 tablespoons olive oil
4 oz. cheese
2 tablespoons chopped fresh basil
salt and black pepper

Peel the potatoes and slice very thinly with a sharp knife. Place them in a bowl and cover with cold water. Allow to stand for about 10 mins. Drain. Peel and slice the onions. Heat the oil in a large frying pan over a medium heat. Add the onions and sauté for 2 mins. Add the potatoes and cook for 15-20 mins, turning frequently until golden and tender. Grate the cheese over the top and cook for 2 mins, without stirring, until the cheese melts. Season and serve.

# PORK SUPREME

1lb lean pork, cubed
1 onion, chopped
1 red or green pepper, chopped
2 sticks celery, chopped
¼ lb mushrooms, sliced
1 small packet peas
2 tablespoons single cream
½ pint of stock
1½ oz. flour
salt and pepper

Toss pork in seasoned flour and fry in oil until browned on all sides. Place in an ovenproof casserole dish. Add onion, celery, pepper and stock. Cover and put into oven for 70-90 mins at gas mark 4, 350°F, 180°C. 15 mins before the end of cooking time, add peas and mushrooms. Just before serving stir in cream. Serve with boiled rice.

31

# CHICKEN AND VEGETABLE STIR-FRY

2 tablespoons cooking oil
4 spring onions, trim & cut into short lengths
2 cloves garlic, crushed
1" fresh root ginger, peeled and sliced
2 skinless chicken fillets, cut into strips
1 tablespoon cornflour
2 courgettes, cut into short lengths
1 red pepper, deseeded and cubed
2 oz. mushrooms, wiped and sliced
2 oz. beansprouts
4 tablespoons orange juice
3 tablespoons dry sherry
good dash of soy sauce
salt and pepper

Heat oil, and fry onions, garlic and ginger. Dip chicken into cornflour, add to pan and cook. Add courgettes, red pepper, mushrooms and beansprouts. Cook for 1 min. Add orange juice, sherry and soy sauce. Cook for a further min, or until chicken is thoroughly cooked and the sauce has thickened. Season and serve with boiled rice.

# CORONATION STREET HOTPOT

8 lamb chops
2 lambs kidneys, sliced
2 onions, peeled and sliced
8 oz. carrots, peeled and sliced
1½lb potatoes, peeled and sliced
salt and black pepper
½ pint of stock
parsley
knob of butter

Layer meat and vegetables in a large casserole dish. Season with salt and pepper. Finish with a layer of over lapping potatoes. Dot with butter. Pour the stock over. Cover and cook in oven at gas mark 160°C for 2 hours. Remove lid and turn heat up to gas mark 6, 400°F, 200°C to brown the top. Sprinkle with chopped parsley before serving.

*Handy Hints*

*In frosty weather put a little methylated spirits on the heels or soles of footwear to stop slipping.*

*Clothing picks up smoky smells if the wearer has been in the company of smokers for some time, when returning home place the garment on a warm radiator to get rid of the smell.*

*When preparing to cut the grass for the first time in a season, use an old blade in the mower so any stones or objects in the grass from the winter don't break a new blade.*

# MEDITERRANEAN LAMB

1 tablespoon olive oil
1 ½ lb cubed lamb
1 large onion, chopped
1 large green pepper, deseeded and sliced
1 dessert spoon flour
1 can chicken peas
16 fl ozs. stock
1 teaspoon all spice
1 tablespoon lemon juice
4 oz. dried apricots
salt and black pepper

Cooking Temperature – gas mark 4, 350°F, 180°C
Heat oil in flameproof casserole on frying pan. Brown lamb a little at a time over a high heat. Remove and keep warm. Add onion and pepper to casserole and sauté until soft. Return meat to pan. Add flour, stir, add chickpeas, all spice, salt and pepper and just enough stock to cover the meat. Cover and bake for 1 hour then add apricots and lemon juice. Add a little more stock if the sauce is too thick. Return to oven for a further 15 mins.

# HAMBURGERS WITH SAUCE

1lb minced beef
2 onions, chopped
1 dessertspoon tomato puree
2 teaspoons chopped parsley
pinch of garlic salt
1 dessertspoon mustard
2 eggs, beaten

**Southern Style Sauce**
Large tin of tomatoes
1 onion, sliced
1 teaspoon oregano
2 teaspoons chopped parsley
1 small green pepper
1 teaspoon sugar
seasoning

**Mushroom Sauce**
2 oz. mushrooms, chopped
2 rashers bacon, chopped
½ oz. butter
1 teaspoon sugar
½ tin mushroom soup

Mix all ingredients and shape into 4 burgers

**Southern Style Sauce**
Put all ingredients into pan and simmer for 10-12 minutes

**Mushroom Sauce**
Fry mushroom and bacon in butter until soft. Add soup.

*H**andy** **H**ints* When going shopping keep a cool-box in the car boot for cold and frozen shopping items.

*A wristwatch that has a plastic face with scratches can be helped with a little windolene and polished.*

33

# SWEET AND SOUR SAUSAGES

8 skinless sausages
1 onion, sliced
1 small can pineapple
1 chicken stock cube
2 tablespoons oil
1 green pepper, sliced
1 tablespoon worcester sauce
1 large tomato skinned
1 tablespoon sweet chutney

Cut sausages into 2 pieces, heat oil and brown sausages. Add onion, pepper and fry for 2 mins. Drain pineapple, cut into four pieces. Save juice make it up to _ pint with water. Blend cornflour with a little of juice to a smooth paste, add rest of juice. Add to the pan, crumble in stock cube, add Worcester sauce and chutney. Cut pineapple and tomato into pieces and add. Stir well. Cook slowly for 10 minutes.

# BLUE CHEESE BITES

3 oz. butter
3 oz. plain flour
3 oz. blue cheese crumbled
2 tablespoons celery seeds
3 tablespoons natural yoghurt
seasoning
2 tablespoons beaten egg

Rub the butter into the flour and mix in the cheese. Add the egg and seasoning, chill the dough for approx. 1 hour. Roll out and cut into rounds using a small pastry cutter. Brush with yoghurt and sprinkle with celery seeds. Bake for 12 mins until crisp at gas mark 4, 350°F, 180°C. Serve as nibbles or with dips.

# STUFFING FOR 2 PORK FILLETS

4 oz. couscous
½ pt boiling water
4 oz. golden sultanas
4 oz. apricots dried
1 cup sherry
sprinkling of demerara sugar
2 tablespoons parsley
½ egg beaten or honey
**Pork Fillet Sauce**
2 tablespoons pork juice
2oz. demerara sugar

Pour water over couscous and leave until it doubles in size. Mix all the ingredients and leave to marinade. Add above to couscous but don't add liquid. Leave to side. Blend ingredients above with the rest. Split pork fillets, add stuffing and secure. Bake at gas mark 4, 350°C, 180°C for one and a half hours.
**Pork Fillet Sauce**
Blend together in saucepan. Add can of apricots halves and juice from marinade and bring to boil.

# Desserts

# AFTER EIGHT CHEESECAKE

**Base**
6 oz. Digestive biscuits
3 oz. butter
**Filling**
2 teaspoons cocoa powder
¼ cup icing sugar
1 teaspoon vanilla essence
1 large philadelphia cheese
1 box after eight mints
1½ pt whipped cream

Crush digestive biscuits and add melted butter. Spread in grease flan dish and leave in fridge. Cream cheese, sugar and vanilla, add cocoa powder and add whipped cream. Spread over base and leave in fridge. Melt after eights with 2 tablespoons of water at a low heat and spread over filling. Cream cheese, sugar and vanilla and add whipped cream. Spread over base and leave in fridge. Melt after eights with 2 tablespoons of water at a low heat and spread over filling.

# CARAMELISED CREAM TARTLETS

Makes 6
**Pastry**
6 oz. plain flour
Water
3 oz. margarine
1 oz. caster sugar
**Filling**
4 egg yolks
1 tsp vanilla essence
1½ oz. caster sugar
Demerara sugar for sprinkling
14 fl ozs. double cream

To make pastry place flour and sugar in bowl and rub in with finger tips. Add water and knead. Roll out the dough to line 6, 4 inch tart tins. Pick the bottoms of the pastry with a fork. Bake in oven for 15 minutes at gas mark 5, 375°F, 190°C. Meanwhile make the filling, in a bowl, beat the egg yolks and sugar until pale. Heat the cream and vanilla essence in a pan until just below boiling point, then pour it onto the egg mixture whisking constantly. Return the mixture to a clean pan and bring just to boil stirring until thick. Do not allow to boil or it will curdle. Leave the mixture to cool slightly then pour into the tart tins. Leave to cool and then leave to chill overnight. Sprinkle the tarts wit the sugar. Place under a preheated hot grill for a few minutes. Leave to cool, then chill for 2 hours before serving.

 *Handy Hints*

*A kettle of boiling water (used carefully) can help get rid of unsightly weeds in the patio.*

*Two teaspoons of honey in nighttime tea should help with a cough free night.*

*Musty smells in the wardrobe or drawers can be cleared with a few drops of vanilla essence.*

# CHERRY IN THE CLOUD

**Meringue ingredients**
3 eggs
6 oz. caster sugar
**Filling ingredients**
½ pkt. marshmallows chopped
½ carton natural yoghurt
1 pkt. philadelphia cheese
Small carton cream whipped
½ cup sugar
1 pkt. cherry pie filling

Beat egg whites until stiff and add caster sugar by tablespoons and beat until stiff. Line swiss roll tin with parchment paper and bake meringue in oven at gas mark2, 300°F, 150°C for 1 hour until cooked. Cool.
Cream cheese and sugar and add other ingredients. Spread on meringue and leave overnight. Cover with cherry pie filling.


# LEMON AND PINEAPPLE CRUMBLE

**Filling**
1 sachet royal lemon pie filling
1 egg
1 medium tin pineapple pieces

**Ingredients for crumble**
3 oz. butter
5 oz. plain flour
3 oz. caster sugar

Strain pineapple and add water to make half a pint. Empty powder into saucepan. Blend in the half pint of liquid and one well-beaten egg. Cook, stirring continuously until mixture boils up once. Add pineapple pieces. Pour into 2 pt. oval dish.
Crumble
Rub butter into flour. Stir in sugar. Spread over the filling. Bake in a fairly hot oven for 20-30 minutes.

 *Handy Hints*

*If clothes cling to the wearer spray the inside of the garment with hair spray, as it is anti-static.*

*Spread some chopped up banana skins around rose bushes as it is good fertiliser and helps guard against greenfly.*

*Bananas with the fruit salad? First soak them in their skins in cold water for half an hour as this will help prevent discolouring.*

# ROLLED PAVLOVA

4 egg whites
2 teaspoons vinegar
8 oz. caster sugar
1 teaspoon cornflour

**Filling**
1 small tin condensed milk
Rind and juice of lemon
½ pt. Cream

Beat egg whites until stiff. Continue beating and add cornflour, vinegar and 6 tablespoons castor sugar. Beat until glossy. Fold in remaining sugar. Spread mixture onto lined swiss roll tin , greased and wet with water. Sprinkle with coconut or nuts. Bake in oven at gas mark 2, 300°F, 150°C for 20–25 minutes.
Whip cream and add condensed milk and add rind and juice of lemon and fill rolled pavlova when cool.


# LITTLE STICKY TOFFEE PUDDINGS WITH PECAN TOFFEE SAUCE

**Ingredients for toffee puddings**
3 oz. butter at room temperature
2 eggs beaten
5 oz. caster sugar
6 oz. self-raising flour
6 oz. stoned dates chopped
6 fl ozs. boiling water
½ teaspoon vanilla essence
2 teaspoons coffee essence
¾ teaspoon bi-carbonate soda

**Ingredients for sauce**
6 oz. soft brown sugar
4 oz. butter
6 tablespoons of whipping cream
1 oz. pecan nuts, chopped

Put chopped dates in a bowl and pour boiling water over them then add vanilla, coffee essence and bi-carbonate of soda and leave to the side. Next cream the butter and sugar together. Add beaten eggs one at a time. After that carefully fold in the sifted flour and then fold into date mixture. Divide mixture into 8 greased ramekin dishes and bake in centre of oven for 25 minutes at gas mark 4, 350°F, 180°C. Take puddings out of ramekin dishes before serving. Can be cooked beforehand and reheated by putting them individually onto a baking tray in oven at a low heat. Suitable for freezing.
Put sugar and butter into saucepan and heat gently until sugar is dissolved. Stir in cream and add nuts.


# CITRUS FREEZE

2 eggs separated
¼ pt whipping cream
2 oz. caster sugar
5 small flakes
7 oz. condensed milk
1 lemon rind and juice
2 limes rind and juice

Whisk the egg yolks, condensed milk and cream together. Add rind and juice of lemon and limes to mixture. Whisk egg whites stiffly in separate bowl. And add sugar and continue whisking until stiff. Fold into mixture with 5 roughly flakes. Line 1lb loaf tin with cling film and pour mixture into tin and freeze until hard. Lift out of freezer 5 mins before hand and decorate.

# WALNUT PUDDING

**Butterscotch sauce**
1½ oz./40 g light brown sugar
1½ oz./40 g golden syrup
2 oz./50 g butter or margarine
2 oz./50g walnut halves

**Walnut pudding**
6 oz./175 g butter or marg., softened
½ teaspoon vanilla essence
6 oz./175 g light brown sugar
3 eggs, size 3
6 oz./175 g self-raising flour
3 oz./75g shelled walnuts ground

Grease a two and a half pt. pudding basin. Place all the ingredients for the butterscotch sauce, except the walnuts halves in a small saucepan and heat gently until they melt. Stir occasionally to prevent the mixture sticking. Turn up the heat and simmer for 1-2 mins until the mixture is thick and bubbling. Pour the butterscotch sauce in a thin stream over the base of the prepared pudding basin. Arrange the walnut halves over the butterscotch sauce, covering the base evenly, then set the bowl aside while you prepare the walnut sponge pudding mixture. The butterscotch sauce will set as it cools.

For pudding mixture place the fat and sugar in the bowl and cream together until light and fluffy. Whisk in the eggs, one at a time, adding a little of the flour to prevent curdling. Add the shelled ground walnuts and vanilla essence then sieve in remaining flour. Using a metal spoon, carefully fold in the dry ingredients until everything is well combined, taking care not to over-mix. Spoon the mixture into the pudding basin on top of the butterscotch and walnuts. Smooth the top with a palette knife.

Fold a pleat in the centre of a square of greaseproof paper place over the basin and secure with string. Cover with foil and stand basin in a large saucepan. Steam for one and a half to two hours.


# CHOCOLATE MOUSSE

220g milk chocolate
30g sugar
4 eggs

Whisk egg yolks and blend into melted chocolate. Whisk white of eggs with sugar until stiff. Blend into egg yolks. Pour into individual dishes and top with cream.

# RED FRUIT SALAD AND CRUNCHIE YOGHURT CREAM

1 can (425g) black cherries, drained and juice reserved
¼ pint apple juice
1lb firm pears
8 oz. frozen raspberries
1 packet frozen summer fruits
6 oz. black grapes halved and seeded
**CRUNCHIE YOGHURT CREAM**
1 crunchie bar
1 small carton of cream
1 small natural yoghurt

Place cherries in serving bowl. Put cherry juice in saucepan with apple juice. Peel core and slice pears add to the pan. Bring to the boil and simmer 3-4 mins. Add contents of pan to the cherries. Sprinkle frozen fruit over the warm fruit and leave at room temperature till thawed. Finally add grapes and mix well and chill until required.

**CRUNCHIE YOGHURT CREAM**
Whip small carton of cream, add 1 small natural yoghurt, crush crunchie bar and fold into cream and yoghurt.

# APRICOT BAKEWELL TART

4 oz. shortcrust pastry
2 tablespoons apricot jam
tin of apricots
In a bowl, beat together:
2 oz. marg.
2 oz. sugar,
2 oz. ground rice
1 oz. ground almonds
1 egg
2 teaspoons almond essence.

Cooking Temperature – gas mark 4, 350°F, 180°C
Line a 7" sandwich tin with 4 oz. shortcrust pastry. Spread with 2 tablespoons apricot jam. Cover with tinned, drained apricots Spread the mixture over the apricots and bake for 40 minutes. Serve hot with custard, or cold with whipped cream.

# PEAR & CHERRY CRUMBLE

**Base**
6 oz. Shortcrust pastry to line a flan case.
**Filling**
1 can cherry pie filling.
2 fresh pears, peeled, cored and sliced.
**Topping**
2 oz. marg.
3 oz. plain flour
pinch salt
2 oz. demerara sugar
2 oz. walnuts or almonds

Put cherries and pears into the flan case. Rub marg. into flour and then add other ingredients. Sprinkle over filling. Bake at gas mark 4, 350°F, 180° C for 30-40 minutes.

# BREAD & BUTTER PUDDING

8 oz. brown bread
2 oz. butter
8 oz. dried fruit (Sultanas & Raisins)
2 oz. cherries
2 tablespoon marmalade
2 eggs, beaten
¾ pint milk
½ teaspoon mixed spice
3 oz. soft brown sugar
2 oz. flaked almonds

Butter bread and cut into cubes. Put into a casserole dish. Mix rest of ingredients together and pour over bread. Sprinkle flaked almonds over top. Leave to sit for at least Ω an hour before putting into oven. Bake for 30-35 minutes at gas mark 5, 375°F, 190°C. Serve with custard.

# CHOCOLATE CHEESE CAKE

**Base**
8 oz. digestive biscuits
4 oz. butter, melted
**Filling**
2* 7 oz. bars fruit and nut chocolate
8 oz. butter softened
8 oz. caster sugar
12 oz. cream cheese
2 tablespoons cocoa powder

Crush biscuits and stir in melted butter, and turn into spring form cake tin. Beat butter, sugar until creamy, beat in cream cheese. Melt chocolate and spoon into cheese mixture. Leave overnight. Sift cocoa over top before serving.

# PAN COOKED APPLE CRUMBLE

4½ oz. plain flour
2 tablespoons grated lemon grind
pinch of salt
3½ oz. chilled butter
2½ oz. soft brown sugar
5 apples
1 tablespoon golden syrup

In a large bowl, mix together the flour, lemon rind and salt. Cut 2Ω oz. butter into pieces. Rub into the flour mixture with your fingertips to form coarse crumbs. Stir in sugar. Put mixture in the freezer for 20 mins. Meanwhile, peel, core and chop the apples. Melt the remaining butter in a pan. Add the apples and cook, stirring regularly, for 10 mins. Cover and cook for 5-10 mins, or until tender. Add the golden syrup. Increase the heat and cook until the apples start to caramelise. Transfer the apples to a plate and keep warm. Wipe the pan clean. Set pan over a medium heat. Add crumble. Cook for 5 mins, without stirring, until golden. Spoon the apples into 4 bowls and top with crumble. Serve.

# RASPBERRY ROLL

1 jam swiss roll
1 medium tin raspberries
1 large carton whipping cream

Cut the jam roll in half lengthways. Drain the raspberries and spoon the juice over each section. Place the raspberries on top of one section and cover with the other half. Cover the entire roll with cream and chill for 2 hours. Serve in slices.

---

---

# LEMON SOUFFLÉ

4 eggs, separated
4 oz. caster sugar
Finely grated rind of 2 lemons
Juice of 3 lemons
2 tablespoons water
½ oz. gelatine (sachet)
¼ pt double cream

Place the egg yolks, sugar, lemon rind and juice in a bowl and set over a pan of simmering water. Whisk until thick, creamy and pale in colour then remove from the saucepan. Place the water in a small bowl, sprinkle the gelatine over, stir once and leave until spongy. Place the bowl in a pan of hot water and stir until dissolved. Strain into the lemon mixture and stir well. Whip the cream until it is just standing in peaks. Whisk the egg whites until stiff, and with a metal spoon fold the cream and then the egg whites into the lemon mixture. Pour immediately into the prepared dish. This recipe is time consuming but well worth the effort.

# GINGER ROLL

1 pkt. ginger biscuits
1 carton pure orange juice
1 large carton double cream

Whip the cream. Dip two biscuits in orange juice and sandwich together with cream. Continue to do this until all the biscuits are used and a log shape is achieved. Cover the log with cream and chill for 2 hours.

# STRAWBERRY SOUFFLÉ

3 tablespoons water
1 tablespoon gelatine
¼ pt strawberry puree made from
fresh, frozen or canned
2 teaspoons lemon juice
2 oz. icing sugar, sifted
¼ pt double cream
3 egg whites

Place the water in a small bowl, sprinkle in the gelatine, stir once and leave until spongy. Place the bowl in a pan of hot water and stir until dissolved. Strain the gelatine into the fruit puree and add the lemon juice and sugar. Taste and add more sugar if necessary. Leave the puree in a cool place, stirring occasionally, until it is just beginning to set. Whip the cream until it is just standing in peaks. Please the egg whites in a clean dry bowl and whisk until stiff. Gently fold the cream and then the egg whites into the puree. Pour into the prepared dish.

# MAPLE PECAN ICE CREAM WITH BUTTERSCOTCH SAUCE

2 oz. sugar
½ pt evaporated milk
¼ pt maple syrup
10 fl ozs. whipping cream
2 oz. pecan nuts, chopped

**Butterscotch Sauce**
1 oz. marg.
2 tablespoons brown sugar
1 tablespoon syrup

Dissolve icing sugar into evaporated milk. Add maple syrup and mix well. Lightly whip cream and fold into the mixture. Place in the freezer until mushy. Once the mixture has reached this point beat well, fold in pecan nuts and return to the freezer until firm.

**Butterscotch Sauce**
Melt marg., add brown sugar and syrup in a saucepan until well blended. Boil for 1 minute then serve poured over scoops of ice cream.

# LEMON SYLLABUB

¼ pint pure apple juice
2 tablespoons lemon juice
2 teaspoons rind of lemon
3 oz. sugar
½ pint double cream

Put all ingredients into a bowl. Whisk until thick, 2-3 mins, spoon into individual serving dishes. Chill for several hours. Serve with shortbread biscuits.

 *Handy Hints*   *Those concerned at their full name and address on luggage being visible in airports for 'would be' burglars can reduce the risk by only using their postcodes.*

# RASPBERRY DELIGHT

¼ pt double cream
¼ pint yoghurt
8 oz. raspberries

Whip cream and yoghurt until fairly stiff. Fold in raspberries. Spoon into 4 individual serving dishes. Decorate with raspberries.

# FRUIT FOOL

1lb fruit
sugar to taste
¼ pt custard
¼ pt double cream
lemon juice
colouring (optional)
nuts, chopped

Stew fruit in very little water, with the sugar. Sieve or puree fruit. Fold the puree into custard and cream. Add a few drops of lemon juice and extra sugar, if required. Add colouring (red or green according to the fruit used). Turn into individual serving dishes. Chill in fridge. Decorate with chopped nuts. Serve with shortbread or sponge fingers.

# CHRISTMAS PUDDING

8 oz. butter or marg.
4 eggs
8 oz. brown sugar
8 oz. raisins
2 oz. whole almonds, chopped
8 oz. breadcrumbs
2 oz. peel
1 lemon
1 orange
2 oz. cherries
2 oz. ground almonds

Steep fruit in juice and rind of oranges and lemon overnight. Cream marg. or butter with sugar. Add eggs slowly then breadcrumbs. Add remainder of dry ingredients. Put into large greased bowl and cover with tin foil. Steam for 3 hours.

# ORANGE BOODLE

2 large oranges
½ pt double dairy cream
1 oz. caster sugar
2 teaspoons lemon juice
12 sponge finger biscuits

Grate the rind of 1 orange into a bowl. Cut 4 thin slices of ungrated orange for decoration, then cut each orange in half and squeeze the juice. Stir orange rind, juice, sugar into soured cream. Crumble 1 sponge finger into the bottom of each 4 glasses and arrange 2 sponge fingers on the inside. Pour in cream mixture and chill well. Decorate with halved slices of oranges.

# SICILIAN CHOCOLATE PIE

12 oz. ricotta or low-fat curd cheese
3 oz. caster sugar
4 oz. cottage cheese
2 oz. preserved orange peel
pinch of salt
22cm baked pastry case
3 tablespoons cognac or rum
grated chocolate to decorate
2 oz. bitter chocolate
3 tablespoons apricot jam

Sieve the cheeses and salt into a bowl. Stir in the cognac or rum lightly. Stir or fold in the sugar and chocolate. Chop the peel finely and stir into the cheese mixture. Chill for at least 1 hour. Heat the apricot jam in a small pan until liquid, then brush over the inside of the pastry case. Fill the case with the cheese mixture. Chill until needed. Scatter grated chocolate and chopped peel over the pie before serving.

# SNOW CAKE

1 small tin Ideal milk
1 tin mandarin oranges
¼ cup juice from oranges
¾ cup caster sugar
3 teaspoons gelatine

Whisk milk until thick. Dissolve gelatine in fruit juice. Whisk sugar into milk. Add gelatine. Fold in oranges. Grease a cake tin lightly with butter. Coat with coconut. Pour in milk mixture. Leave to set in fridge. Decorate with whipped cream before serving. This dessert can be prepared the day before.

# CRAFTY TIRAMISU

1 tablespoon coffee
12 oz. mascapone cheese
3 oz. icing sugar
2 eggs separated
8-10 boudoir biscuits
2 choc flakes crumbled
1 large carton cream

Pour 5 fl ozs. of boiling water over coffee, add 2 tablespoons of icing sugar and stir to dissolve. Put layer of biscuits (sugar side up) in 1 pint dish. Pour all of the coffee mix over the biscuits. Beat cheese, egg yolks and remaining icing sugar together. Whisk egg white until stiff and fold into cheese mixture. Crumble in 1 choc flake. Pile mixture over biscuits and smooth down. Whip cream and put over top of mixture and crumble

---

*H*andy *H*ints  *If going away on a prolonged holiday or business trip and concerned about the staleness of the air in a house not going to be lived in, place a sprig of mint in a jar of water as this will keep a fresh aroma for weeks.*

# Cakes

◆◆◆◆◆◆◆◆◆◆◆◆◆◆◆◆◆◆◆◆◆◆◆◆◆◆◆◆◆◆◆◆◆◆◆◆

# CHOCOLATE CAKE

8 oz. soft marg.
1oz. or less of cocoa
8 oz. caster sugar
2 tablespoons warm nearly boiling water
8 oz. self-raising flour
4 eggs
1 level teaspoon baking powder
**Filling**
4 oz. chocolate
5 oz. icing sugar
4 oz. butter or marg.
2 tablespoons milk

Beat marg., sugar, flour, cocoa and eggs for 5 mins. Lastly beat in baking powder. Put into prepared sandwich tins. Bake at gas mark 6, 400°F, 200°C for approx. 35 minutes.
**Filling**
Place chocolate and milk in small saucepan. Heat gradually until chocolates melts. Pour over creamed butter and sugar and whisk up quickly. Spread mixture over top and middles of cakes.


# GUM GUM CAKES

3 oz. brown sugar
9 oz. self-raising flour
4½ oz. marg.
1½ teaspoon vanilla essence
3 eggs (yolks)
**Filling**
3 egg whites
1 oz. chopped walnuts
4 oz. caster sugar
1 oz. chopped cherries

Cream together sugar and marg. Add beaten egg yolks, flour and vanilla essence. Place in greased swiss roll tin and flatten.
**Filling**
Beat egg whites till stiff, gradually fold in sugar, nuts and cherries. Spread evenly over base. Bake in oven at gas mark 5, 375°F, 190°C for 20-25 mins.

# BOILED CAKE

1 teacups raisins
6 oz. marg.
1½ teacups sultanas
2/3 eggs
1½ teacups sugar
cherries
1½ teacups water
½ teaspoon salt
3½ teacups plain flour
½ teaspoon ginger
1 ½ teaspoon mixed spice
1½ teaspoon baking soda

Boil fruit, water, sugar and marg. together for 20 mins. Cool. Add other ingredients. Bake in a moderate oven at gas mark 4, 350°F, 180°C for 1 _ hours and then at gas mark 3, 325°F, 170°C for _ hour.


# BANANA CAKE

4 oz. polyunsaturated marg.
1lb peeled ripe bananas, mashed
2 oz. sugar
4 oz. wholemeal flour
1 teaspoon vanilla
4 oz. white flour
1 large egg, well beaten
2 teaspoons baking powder
oil, for greasing

Cooking Temperature – gas mark 4, 350°F, 180°C
Place the marg. and sugar in a bowl with the vanilla, egg, bananas, flour and baking powder. Beat well with a wooden spoon until the mixture is thoroughly blended. Pour the mixture into an oiled 1kg / 2lb loaf tin. Bake in oven for 1 hour, or until a skewer inserted in the centre comes out clean. Turn out onto a wire rack to cool.


# SIMPLE ALL-IN-ONE FRUIT CAKE

12 oz. self-raising flour
4 oz. dried apricots, chopped
6 oz. marg.
6 oz. sultanas
6 oz. soft brown sugar
4 oz. cherries, halved

Cooking Temperature – gas mark 3, 325°F, 170°C
Sift the flour into a large bowl. Add the remaining ingredients, beat the mixture for 2-3 mins until slightly glossy and lighter in colour. Scrape the mixture into the prepared tin with a spatula, level the top and bake for one and a half hours. Allow the cake to cool in the tin for 3 mins and then turn out onto a wire rack and leave to cool.

# SICILIAN CHOCOLATE PIE

12 oz. ricotta or low-fat curd cheese
3 oz. caster sugar
4 oz. cottage cheese
2 oz. preserved orange peel
pinch of salt
22cm baked pastry case
3 tablespoons cognac or rum
grated chocolate to decorate
2 oz. bitter chocolate
3 tablespoons apricot jam

Sieve the cheeses and salt into a bowl. Stir in the cognac or rum lightly. Stir or fold in the sugar and chocolate. Chop the peel finely and stir into the cheese mixture. Chill for at least 1 hour. Heat the apricot jam in a small pan until liquid, then brush over the inside of the pastry case. Fill the case with the cheese mixture. Chill until needed. Scatter grated chocolate and chopped peel over the pie before serving.


# THE FAMILY WEDDING CAKE

1lb butter
8 eggs
1lb currants
1½ lbs sultanas
1lb raisins
½ lb mixed peel
14 oz. cherries
¼ lb glaze pineapple
6 oz. whole almonds
1lb soft brown sugar or white sugar
1lb plain flour
1 teaspoon nutmeg
1½ teaspoons mixed spice
½ lb ground almonds
Rind and juice of 1 lemon
Rind and juice of 3 small oranges
Pinch of salt
½ teaspoon baking powder if wished
N.B. keep all fruit large

This mixture makes bottom tier and separate mixture will make middle tier and top tier Prepare fruit and add the rind and juice of lemon and oranges. Leave overnight to absorb the juice. Cream butter and sugar. Add eggs, fruit and mix well with hands. Add flour, salt and spices and baking powder. Mix well with hands. Bake in oven in a large lined cake tin at gas mark 1, 275°F, 140°C for about 1 hour and gradually lower to 200°F. Bake for approx 6 hours.

# CHOCOLATE AND STRAWBERRY GATEAU

7 oz. self-raising flour
1 oz. cocoa powder
6 oz. butter
6 oz. soft brown sugar
3 eggs
4 oz. plain chocolate melted
**Filling**
15 fl ozs. double cream
8 oz. plain chocolate
4 oz. strawberries, sliced
4 oz. plain chocolate grated

Cooking Temperature – gas mark 4, 350°F, 180°C
Sift the flour and cocoa powder into a bowl and reserve. Place the butter and sugar in a large bowl and cream with an electric whisk until light and fluffy. Whisk the eggs lightly, then beat into the mixture, a little at a time, beating well after each addition. Beat in the chocolate. Bake for 25-30 mins. Put a third of the cream into a pan with the chocolate and heat gently, stirring, until melted. Cool, then whisk until thick and glossy. Whip the remaining cream and fold half into the chocolate mixture. Spoon the remaining cream into a piping bag fitted with a star nozzle and reserve. Use half the chocolate cream, topped with most of the strawberries, to sandwich the cakes together. Spread the remaining chocolate cream on top and decorate with rosettes of whipped cream, grated chocolate and the remaining berries. Keep cool and serve within 2 hours.

# CREAMED SPONGE

6 oz. self-raising flour
6 oz. caster sugar
6 oz. butter / marg.
3 eggs

Cooking Temperature – gas mark 4, 350°F, 180°C
Sift the flour into a bowl and reserve. Place the butter and sugar in a large bowl and cream with an electric whisk until light and fluffy. Whisk the eggs lightly, then beat into the mixture, a little at a time, beating well after each addition. If the mixture shows signs of curdling, add a spoonful of flour and beat in. Bake for 25-30 mins. Allow the cake to cool in the tin for 1 min and then turn out onto wire rack. Leave the cake to cool completely.

# LEMON REFRIGERATOR CAKE

4 oz. butter
6 oz. caster sugar
4 eggs
rind and juice of 1 lemon
18 sponge fingers

whipped cream or chocolate sauce

Cream the butter and sugar until very white and light. Beat in egg yolks, grated rind and juice of the lemon. Fold in stiffly beaten egg whites. Split sponge fingers into 2 or 3 layers and line oblong tin or pie dish with some of them. Fill with alternate layers of sponge and lemon mixture finishing with sponge. Cover and chill 12-24 hours. Turn out and cut into slices. Serve with cream or chocolate sauce.


# SNOW CAKE

1 small tin Ideal milk
1 tin mandarin oranges
¾ cup juice from oranges
¾ cup caster sugar
3 teaspoons gelatine

Whisk milk until thick. Dissolve gelatine in fruit juice. Whisk sugar into milk. Add gelatine. Fold in oranges. Grease a cake tin lightly with butter. Coat with coconut. Pour in milk mixture. Leave to set in fridge. Decorate with whipped cream before serving. This dessert can be prepared the day before.


# LEMON GATEAU

6 oz. marg.
6 oz. self-raising flour
6 oz. caster sugar
1½ teaspoon baking soda
1 teaspoon finely grated lemon zest
3 large eggs
1 teaspoon lemon juice

Cream fat and sugar until soft and light. Gradually beat in eggs. Sieve flour and baking powder into mixture. Add lemon juice. Put into 2, 7" greased tins. Bake for 18 minutes at gas mark 4, 350°F, 180°C. Blend half lb lemon curd with one quarter pint of whipped cream for filling and top. Decorate with lemon slices.

# PINEAPPLE CAKE WITH A DIFFERENCE

4oz. marg.
12 oz. mixed fruit
6 oz. granulated sugar
1 teaspoon bi-carbonate of soda
12 oz. self-raising flour
2 eggs
1 teaspoon mixed spice
12 oz. crushed pineapple

Put sugar, marg., fruit, pineapple with juice, spice and bi-carbonate of soda into a saucepan and slowly bring to the boil. Boil for 3 mins and allow to cool completely. Add the flour and 2 well-beaten eggs and mix well. Place the mix into a tin (greased and lined with greaseproof paper) and bake for 90 mins at gas mark 2, 300°F, 150°C. Serve with fresh cream.

# CHERRY CAKE

12 oz. plain flour
8 oz. caster sugar
8 oz. marg.
6 oz. glace cherries
2 oz. ground almonds
1 teaspoon almond essence
4 eggs
½ cup milk
2 level teaspoon baking powder

Cream marg. and sugar. Add egg yolks and beat well. Then add flour, milk, ground almonds and essence. Beat egg whites until stiff and fold into mixture. Add baking powder. Turn mixture into a greased and lined 7" cake tin. Bake at gas mark 3, 325°F, 170°C for one and a quarter hours.

# COFFEE SANDWICH

4 oz. sugar
6oz. flour
4 eggs, separated
½ teaspoon baking soda
coffee essence

Beat the egg whites until stiff, add the sugar and then beat again. Stir in yolks and beat until the mixture is thick. Fold in the flour and baking powder, add enough coffee essence to turn the mixture a light brown colour. Bake at gas mark 5, 375°F, 190°C for 20-30 mins.

# SPEEDY ORANGE CAKE

5 oz. self-raising flour
2 eggs
4 oz. caster sugar
1 tablespoon orange juice
3 oz. marg.
rind of 1 orange

Put all the ingredients together in a bowl and cream until softened then beat briskly for 2 mins until light and fluffy. Put into a 7" round tin. Bake at gas mark 4, 350°F, 180°C for 1 hour.

# Tray Bakes

••••••••••••••••••••

# FLAPJACKS

6 oz. marg.
6 oz. porridge oats
4 oz. caster sugar
2 oz. self raising flour
pinch salt

Melt marg. in saucepan over low heat. Stir in sugar until well mixed. Take off heat and stir in oats, salt and flour. Mix well. Turn into greased swiss roll tin and spread level. Bake at gas mark 5, 375°F, 190°C for approx. 20 mins. Cut immediately and leave in tin to cool.

# MOCHA SQUARES

8 oz. marg.
8 oz. granulated sugar
8 oz. self raising flour
5 oz. porridge oats
2 oz. cocoa
**Icing**
1 tablespoon coffee essence
2 oz. marg.
1 tablespoon water
8 oz. icing sugar

Lightly grease tin 13" * 9" with melted fat. Heat marg. gently in pan. Stir in the other ingredients and mix well. Press into prepared tin and bake for 15 mins. Only in centre of oven, gas mark 4, 350°F, 180°C. Cool in tin.

Melt marg. in pan with coffee essence and water. Sift sugar into bowl. Add all melted ingredients and beat well. Pour onto base in tin.

# WALNUT DELIGHTS

2 egg whites
3 oz. caster sugar
3 oz. chopped walnuts
1 oz. ground or chopped almonds
few drops vanilla essence

Beat egg whites slightly then mix in all other ingredients. Cook at 200°F, 100°C for two to two and a half hours.

# QUICK SHORTBREAD

9 oz. plain or self-raising flour
3 oz. caster sugar
3 oz. corn flour
8 oz. butter/marg.
pinch salt

Melt butter. Add to dry ingredients and blend together. Spread on greased swiss roll tin. Fork all over. Bake on middle shelf at gas mark 2, 300°F, 150°C for 1 hour. When cooked sprinkle with caster sugar and cut into fingers while still hot. Place on cooling tray. If liked, the butter may be creamed instead of melted but cook for one and ahalf hours until lightly browned.

# QUICK CURRANT SQUARES

1 large pkt. frozen shortcrust pastry (14 oz.) or equivalent in homemade pastry.
**Filling**
8 oz. currants
2 oz. brown sugaror
8 oz. mixed fruit
2 oz. marg.

Use half pastry to line a large greased swiss roll tin.
Soften marg. and syrup. Mix with sugar and currants. Spread on pastry and cover with remaining half pastry. Brush with cold water and sprinkle with caster sugar. Bake at gas mark 6, 400°F, 200°C for 25-30 mins. Cut into squares when cool.

# PEPPERMINT CHOCOLATE SQUARES

**Base**
4 oz. marg.
2 oz. caster sugar
4 oz. plain flour
2 oz. coconut
1 tablespoon baking powder
1 tablespoon cocoa
2 tablespoons drinking chocolate
**Icing**
3 oz. icing sugar
2 drops peppermint essence
green colouring
2 oz. marg.

Cream marg. and sugar. Add rest of ingredients and mix well. Spread in swiss roll tin. Bake at gas mark 6, 400°F, 200°C. Icing2 oz. marg.

Cream all ingredients together. Spread on cold base and cover with 6 oz. melted chocolate. Cut into squares.

# CARAMEL CRUMBLE

**Base**
3 oz. marg.
6 oz. flour
2 oz. caster sugar
**Filling**
4 oz. marg.
3 oz. caster sugar
2 dessertspoons syrup
1 small tin condensed milk

Rub marg. into flour and sugar till it resembles crumbs. Spread over a greased swiss roll tin and bake at gas mark 4, 350°F, 180°C for 20-25 mins until golden.
**Filling**
Melt marg. sugar and syrup in saucepan. Add condensed milk and bring to the boil for about 5 mins. Spread over base and cover with half a block melted chocolate. Cut into squares when set.


# NUTTY CHERRY FINGERS

6 glace cherries
1 oz. nuts
4 oz. butter
6 oz. plain flour
2 level tablespoons custard powder
3 oz. caster sugar

Heat oven to gas mark 3, 325°F, 160°C. Chop nuts and cherries. Rub butter into flour and custard powder. Stir in sugar, cherries and half the nuts. Press into a swiss roll tin. Press the remaining nuts on top and bake towards the top of the oven for 25-30 mins. Sprinkle with caster sugar and cut into fingers. Leave to cool in tin.


# BISCUIT MALLOWS

**Base**
4 wheetabix
4 oz. marg.
1 cup coconut
1 cup self raising flour
½ cup sugar
pinch salt
**Topping**
1 cup sugar
¼ cup water
1 pkt. gelatine

Crush wheetabix and add with all other ingredients to melted marg. Spread on swiss roll tin. Bake at gas mark 4, 350°F, 180°C for 15-20 mins. Cool.
**Topping**
Put all in saucepan and boil for 3 mins. Cool and beat until white and thick. Spread over base and allow to set.

# CHINESE CHEWS

8 oz. dates
3 oz. marg.
4.oz chopped nuts
4 oz. sugar
3 oz. flour
2 eggs
a little almond essence

Chop nuts and dates.
Cream marg. and sugar. Beat in eggs. Fold in flour and add nuts and dates. Pour into greased swiss roll tin and bake at gas mark 4. 350°F, 180°C for about 30 mins. Cool in tin and cut into fingers.


# TOFFEE BARS

**Base**
4 oz. butter
3 oz. brown sugar
1 egg yolk
2 oz. plain flour
2 oz. porridge oats
**Topping**
3 oz. plain chocolate
1 tablespoon butter
chopped walnuts

Beat together butter, sugar and egg yolk until smooth. Add flour and oats and stir well. Press mixture into greased swiss roll tin. Bake for 15 mins. At gas mark 5, 375°F, 190°C. Cool slightly.
**Topping**
Melt chocolate and butter over hot water. Spread over warm base and decorate with nuts. Cut into bars while warm. Leave to cool in tin.


# BRIDES SLICES

4 oz. marg.
9 oz. crushed digestive biscuits
3 oz. caster sugar
6 oz. sultanas
2 small eggs beaten
2 oz. cherries
1 teaspoon mixed spice

Melt marg. and sugar. Stir in other ingredients. Press into swiss roll tin. Bake at gas mark 4, 350°F, 180°C for approx. 20 mins. Ice with water icing when cold and cut into squares.

# QUICK BAKE TRAY

1 cup crushed cornflakes
6 oz. marg.
1 cup self-raising flour
1 tablespoon drinking chocolate
1 cup coconut
½ cup sugar

Mix dry ingredients. Melt marg. and pour over dry ingredients. Mix well. Put into ungreased swiss roll tin. Bake 20 mins at gas mark 4, 370°F, 185°C. Melt cooking chocolate and pour over.


# CARAMEL FINGERS

**Shortbread base**
4 oz. marg. or butter
2 oz. caster sugar
6 oz. self-raising flour
**Topping**
4 oz. marg.
4 oz. caster sugar
2 tablespoons syrup
1 small tin condensed milk

Cream butter and sugar. Stir in flour. Spread on a greased swiss roll tin and bake at gas mark 2, 300°F, 150°C for about 1 hour or until firm and golden.
**Topping**
Melt ingredients together in a saucepan. Beat gently at first then boil until the caramel leaves the side of the pan. Keep it well stirred. Pour over shortbread base. When cold, cover over with 4 oz. melted chocolate. Cut into fingers when cold.


# PARADISE SQUARES

Shortcrust pastry
raspberry jam
**Topping**
4 oz. caster sugar
4 oz. marg. 2 oz. cherries
2 oz. ground rice
2 oz. coconut
2 oz. chopped nuts
1 egg

Line a swiss roll tin with pastry and spread with jam.
**Topping**
Cream marg. and sugar and add rest of ingredients. Spread on base and bake at gas mark 4, 350°F, 180°C for 30 mins. Cut into squares.

# LEMON SLICES

6 oz. marg.
3 oz. sugar
6 oz. self-raising flour
2 oz. cornflakes
4 oz. coconut
1 lemon
8 oz. icing sugar
1 dessertspoon custard powder

Cream marg. and sugar and grated lemon rind. Add cornflakes, coconut and flour. Place in swiss roll tin and bake for 25 mins at gas mark 5, 375°F, 190°C. When cold, ice with lemon icing made with icing sugar, custard powder and juice of the lemon.


# ALMOND SLICES

**Base**
8 oz. shortcrust pastry
4 tablespoons apricot jam
**Topping**
4 oz. icing sugar
4 oz. ground almonds
4 oz. caster sugar
2 oz. ground rice
1 egg and 1 egg white
1 tablespoon almond essence
lemon juice
flaked almonds (optional)

Roll out pastry to fit 11" * 7" swiss roll tin. Prick well and spread with jam.
**Topping**
Mix all ingredients together except flake almonds and spread over pastry. If liked, flaked almonds may be sprinkled over mixture before placing in oven. Bake for 10 mins at gas mark 6, 425°F, 210°C then lower to gas mark 4, 350°F, 180°C for a further 10-15 mins until golden.


# NUTTY FUDGE SHORTBREAD

**Base**
4 oz. marg
4 oz. caster sugar.
8 oz. flour
1 egg yolk
**Topping**
3 oz. chopped nuts
6 oz. soft brown sugar
1 egg white

Make shortbread and press into swiss roll tin. Cook slightly at gas mark 3, 320°F, 160°C.
**Topping**
Beat egg white and add sugar and nuts. Spread on top of shortbread base using a little jam. Cook for 20 mins.

# VIENNA TRAY BAKE

**Base**
6 oz. butter
2 oz. icing sugar
4 oz. self-raising flour
2 oz. cornflourpinch salt
few drops of vanilla essence
**Topping**
1 level tablespoon caster sugar
1 oz. flaked almonds

Cream butter until soft then stir in sifted icing sugar, flour and cornflour, salt and vanilla to form a stiff dough. Turn onto a swiss roll tin and sprinkle over sugar and almonds. Bake at gas mark 4, 350°F, 180°C for 20-25 mins until golden. Cut into fingers while warm.


# BUTTERSCOTCH SQUARES

2 oz. butter
3 oz. self-raising flour
4 oz. soft brown sugar
1 level teaspoon vanilla essence
1 large egg
1 oz. chopped walnuts

Melt butter and sugar in a pan over low heat stirring all the time. Mixture will turn a slightly darker brown when ready but do not allow to boil. Cool then beat in egg. Sift flour and stir into mixture with vanilla and nuts. Turn into a well greased shallow seven and a half " square tin and ease it to the sides. Bake at gas mark 4, 350°F, 180°C until it shrinks from the sides – about 30 mins.


# CHERRY CHEWS

**Base**
6 oz. cooking chocolate
**Topping**
4 oz. coconut
4 oz. caster sugar
1 egg
2 oz. cherries

Melt chocolate and line swiss roll tin. Leave to set. Beat egg, add caster sugar, coconut and chopped cherries. Spread over chocolate. Cook at gas mark 3, 325°F, 160°C until golden brown on top. Cut when cool.

# Non Bakes

# WONDER BITES

2 oz. butter
4 oz. icing sugar
1 teaspoon coffee essence
3 oz. desiccated coconut
2 oz. chopped walnuts
3 oz. chopped cherries
6 oz. cooking chocolate for coating

Cream butter and sugar. Add the rest of the ingredients and roll into small balls. Put into fridge to firm while melting chocolate. Coat with chocolate and place on greaseproof paper.

# FUDGE BISCUITS

7 oz. digestive biscuits
4 oz. marg.
6 oz. caster sugar
2 tablespoons syrup
Small tin condensed milk

Melt marg., sugar, syrup and condensed milk and simmer for 5 mins. Turn off heat, add crumbed biscuits and mix well. Put into greased swiss roll tin and cover with chocolate. Place in fridge or cool place to harden.

# LEMON ICED BISCUITS

1pkt. Marie biscuits
3 oz. coconut
4 oz. marg.
1 small tin condensed milk
1 lemon

Crush biscuits. Melt marg. Add condensed milk, then biscuits, coconut and lemon rind. Place on greased swiss roll tin and when set cover with lemon icing using juice of lemon.

# BISCUIT CRUNCH

8 oz. digestive biscuits
2 oz. raisins
2 oz. cherries chopped
2 tablespoons syrup
4 oz. butter
4 oz. block chocolate melted

Crush biscuits in a bowl. Add raisins and cherries. Melt syrup and butter and add to dry ingredients with melted chocolate. Mix well to coat biscuits. Press into swiss roll tin. Chill in fridge for at least an hour.

**Topping**
4 oz. block chocolate
2 oz. butter
6 oz. icing sugar

Melt butter and chocolate. Sift in icing sugar and mix until well blended. Spread over base and fork in lines to decorate. Cut into fingers when cool.

# MALLOW CUSHIONS

4 oz. dark cooking chocolate
1 level tablespoon syrup
2 oz. seedless raisins
1 oz. marg.
4 oz. pink & white marshmallows

Melt chocolate with marg. and sugar. Cut up marshmallows and add. When melted add raisins and biscuits. Press mixture into greased 7"square shallow tin or double mixture into a large swiss roll tin. Put in fridge to set.

# MALLOW / COCONUT FRIDGE ROLL

6 oz. digestive biscuits
8 oz. marshmallows
2 oz. chopped walnuts
2 oz. chopped small cherries
tin condensed milk
coconut to cover

Crush biscuits and put into a bowl. Cut mallows in half and add to biscuits with chopped cherries and walnuts. Mix in condensed milk. Mould into a roll and cover with coconut. Put into fridge until firm. Cut into slices.

# TANGY ORANGE SQUARES

7 oz. rich tea biscuits (crushed)
rind and juice of 1 orange
4 oz. coconut
4 oz. marg.
1 small tin condensed milk
coating chocolate

Mix dry ingredients in a bowl. Add condensed milk, melted marg. and orange juice. Press into greased swiss roll tin. Ice with melted chocolate. Cut into squares when set.

# MINT DIGESTIVES

**Base**
.8 oz. digestive biscuits
4 oz. marg.
2 oz. sugar
1 beaten egg
2 tablespoons drinking chocolate
**Filling**
2 oz. icing sugar
3 oz. marg.
peppermint essence
few drops of green colouring
6 oz. cooking chocolate

Crush biscuits. Melt marg., sugar and drinking chocolate in a saucepan. Add biscuits and well-beaten egg. Press into swiss roll tin. Beat icing sugar, marg., essence and colouring together. Spread over base and cover with melted chocolate. Cut when cool.

# MARS BAR KRISPS

3 cups rice krispies
3 mars bars
2 oz. marg.
coating chocolate

Melt mars bars and marg. in a bowl over hot water. Add rice krispies. Place on a tray and coat with melted chocolate if desired.

# HEDGEHOGS

4oz. marg.
1 cup soft brown sugar
¾ cup mixed fruit
1 egg beaten
½ lb. crushed digestive biscuits
Topping
block chocolate
chopped nuts

Melt marg., sugar and fruit in a saucepan. Cool a little and add beaten egg. Cook 1 min. and add crushed biscuits. Press into swiss roll tin and leave to cool. Spread with melted chocolate and chopped nuts. Cut into squares when cool.

# COFFEE BARS

**Base**
8 oz. digestive biscuits
4 oz. icing sugar
2 tablespoons coffee essence
2 tablespoon ground almonds
1 small tin condensed milk

**Topping**
3 oz. butter
3 oz. icing sugar
4 oz. block chocolate
2 oz. marg.

Crush biscuits. Add all ingredients and mix together. Spread on a swiss roll tin.

**Topping**
Make butter icing by creaming butter and icing sugar until creamy. Spread over base. Melt chocolate with marg. and pour over butter icing. Cut when cool.

# JELLY SQUARES

small tin condensed milk
6 oz. coconut
1 pkt. jelly crystals
coating chocolate

Mix crystals and coconut together. Stir in condensed milk. Press into tray and coat with melted chocolate.

# CRUNCHIES

1 small pkt. rice krispies
4 oz. marshmallows
2 bars toffee
4 oz. marg.

Melt toffee, mallows and marg. in a saucepan. Remove from heat and add krispies. Stir until well coated. Put into greased tins, press down and allow to cool. Cut into squares.

# PEANUT FINGERS

6 oz. rich tea biscuits
1 oz. caster sugar
2 oz. marg.
2 level tablespoons syrup
4 tablespoons peanut butter
12 squares cooking chocolate

Crush biscuits. Put sugar, marg. and syrup in saucepan and stir over low heat until melted. Remove from heat, stir in peanut butter and crushed biscuits. Press into swiss roll tin, leave in a cool place to set and cover with melted chocolate.

# NUTTY FINGERS

1 Mars bar
3 gm rice krispies
1 Snickers bar
2 gm marg.
3 gm chocolate

Melt the mars, snickers and marg. in a pan. Add the rice krispies and spread in a flat tin. Cover with melted chocolate.

# OVALTINE CREAMS

**Base**
7 oz. rich tea biscuits
4 oz. marg.
4 oz. soft brown sugar
2 level tablespoons ovaltine
3 oz. coconut
3 oz. cherries

**Topping ingredients**
10 oz. icing sugar
2 oz. marg.
2 tablespoons custard powder
2 tablespoons boiling water

Melt marg., sugar and ovaltine in saucepan. Add coconut, cherries. Add beaten eggs and cook for $\Omega$ minute in saucepan. Stir in broken biscuits and spread in a swiss roll tin.

**Topping**
Cream together marg. and icing sugar. Mix custard powder and water. In small bowl and then add to marg. and icing sugar. Put mixture over biscuit base and sprinkle with ovaltine.

# CRUNCHY PEANUT BISCUITS

8 oz. cooking chocolate
1 large jar crunch peanut butter
3 oz. marshmallows, cut into small pieces
4 oz. rice krispies
White chocolate for decorating

Melt cooking chocolate and add peanut butter. Cool. Add rice krispies and marshmallows. Spread mixture into swiss roll tin and spread with white chocolate.

*H*andy *Hints*

*Sprinkle a little baking powder in the boiling fat when frying chips, as this should make them brown and crisp.*

*Light coloured shoes can be badly discoloured with black marks; a little nail polish remover will help remove it.*

*When making soup, if too salty place a peeled potato in it, removing before it crumbles. The potato will absorb much of the salt.*

*If soft brown sugar has gone hard, place in a bowl, cover with a damp cloth overnight for morning after soft sugar again.*

*To create a very unusual display with fresh flowers, dissolve a cold water dye in warm water. Leave to cool, before pouring it into a vase. Crush the stems of your flowers and then arrange them in the vase after about two hours the flowers will change colour. The dye gives them a stunning streaked effect.*

# Bread & Scones

◆◆◆◆◆◆◆◆◆◆◆◆◆◆◆◆◆◆◆

# WHEATEN BREAD

125g self-raising flour
½tablespoon baking soda
150g wholemeal flour
50g marg.
1 tablespoon caster sugar
½pt buttermilk

Mix flour (both types), baking soda and sugar in a basin. Add marg. rub in until mixture looks like breadcrumbs. Add buttermilk and mix together. Put into an 8" loaf tin and bake at gas mark 3, 325°F, 170°C for 30-45 mins. Turn out onto a wire rack to cool.

# PANCAKES

2 teacups self-raising flour
3 teaspoons sugar
½teaspoon baking soda
1 tablespoon syrup
2 eggs
sweet milk

Sieve the dry ingredients. Add beaten egg, syrup and enough milk to make a dropping consistency. Put spoonfuls of the mixture onto a hot, lightly greased griddle and cook on both sides.

# WELSH PANCAKES

6 tablespoons plain flour
pinch salt
2-3 tablespoons sour cream
2-3 eggs
2 tablespoons sugar
buttermilk / sweet milk
½tablespoon cream of tartar (dissolved in water)

Put all ingredients into a bowl and make a batter. Drop spoonfuls of the mixture onto a hot griddle and cook on both sides. Serve hot with butter.

# DROP SCONES

8 oz. plain flour
½ teaspoon salt
1 teaspoon baking soda
1 egg
½pt buttermilk

Lightly grease the griddle and heat well. Sift the flour, salt, baking soda. Beat in egg and milk until a batter is formed. Spoon onto the griddle and when bubbles rise to the surface, turn over and cook for a further minute. Serve with butter.

# TEA SCONES

8 oz. soda bread flour
2 oz. marg.
1½ oz. caster sugar
buttermilk to mix

Sieve flour, salt and rub in marg. and sugar. Mix with buttermilk. Roll out $\Omega$ inch thick and cut into rounds. Bake in a hot oven until golden brown.

# POTATO BREAD

1lb peeled potatoes
2 oz. butter
2 level teaspoons salt
4 oz. flour

Cook potatoes in boiling salted water for 20 mins, until soft, drain and mash well. Add salt, butter mix in flour to make a stiff mixture. Turn out on a floured board, knead lightly and roll out to $\sum$ inch thick, cut into shapes. Cook on a greased hot griddle for 4-5 mins on each side until golden brown.

# WHOLEMEAL LOAVES

16 oz. wholemeal flour
3 oz. sugar
10 oz. plain flour
1½ teaspoons baking soda
1 large cup of bran
3 oz. marg.
2/3 of a pint of buttermilk

Cooking temperature – gas mark 6, 400°F, 200°C
Mix all dry ingredients together and rub in marg. Mix in the buttermilk – dough should be stiff. Divide between 2 lb tins and bake for 50 mins.

# SCONES

8 oz. self-raising flour
1½ oz. butter
150 ml milk
1½ tablespoons caster sugar
A pinch of salt

Sift flour in a bowl and rub in butter with fingertips. Next stir in the sugar and salt then take a knife and use it to mix in the milk. At this stage you can add fruit or cherries cut into quarters if desired. Knead the mixture to a soft dough and roll out to $\pi$ inch and cut with pastry cutter. Place scones on a greased baking sheet. Put in oven gas mark 7, 425°F, 220°C for 12–15 minutes until golden brown.

# WHEETABIX BREAD

3 * wheetabix
¾ pt milk
½ lb sultanas
½ lb caster sugar
½lb self-raising flour

Soak wheetabix, sugar & sultanas together in milk overnight. Next morning, stir in flour to mixture. Bake in a 2lb loaf tin at gas mark 4, 350°F, 180°C for 1Ω-2 hours. Turn out onto wire rack and cool.

# QUICK FRUIT LOAF

8 oz. self-raising flour
4 oz. marg.
2 oz. fruit
pinch of salt
1 egg
2 oz. sugar
1 cup milk

Put flour, sugar, and salt in a bowl. Stir in melted marg. and mix all the ingredients together. Pour into a greased and floured tin and bake at gas mark 4, 350°F, 180°C for 45 mins.

# ULSTER FRUIT LOAF

1½lb mixed fruit
2 teaspoons spice
8 oz. moist brown sugar
1lb self-raising flour
1 cup cold tea
1 tablespoon treacle
2 eggs
pinch salt

Soak fruit and sugar overnight in cold tea. Sieve together flour, spice, salt and add to the fruit. Mix in eggs and treacle. Pour into large loaf tin and bake at gas mark 5, 375°F, 190°C for 1 hour. Then reduce heat to gas mark 1, 275°F, 140°C for another hour until firm.

# DATE AND WALNUT LOAF

1lb dates
1lb plain flour
1½ teaspoon baking soda
½lb sugar
2 oz. marg.
2 beaten eggs
pinch salt

Steep dates and baking soda in one and a half cups of boiling water and leave to cool. Rub marg. into flour and add sugar, salt and eggs. Finally add fruit mixture. Put into well greased and lined loaf tin (2lb) and bake at gas mark 4, 350°F, 180°C for 1 hour.

# ALL BRAN LOAF

1 cup demerara sugar
1 cup all bran
1 cup raisins
1 cup sweet milk
1 egg
1 cup self-raising flour

Steep the raisins, all bran, milk and sugar overnight. Next day add 1 well-beaten egg and a cup of self-raising flour. Bake for approx 1 hour at gas mark 5, 375°F, 190°C in a prepared loaf tin.

# TEABRACK

13 oz. packet of mixed fruit
8 oz. brown sugar
10 fl ozs. of hot tea
10 oz. self-raising flour
Good pinch of salt
1 egg
1 teaspoon marmalade
1 oz. chopped nuts (optional)
1 oz. melted marg.

Pour the fruit and sugar into a bowl and pour over the hot tea. Mix well, cover and leave to stand overnight. Preheat oven to gas mark 3, 325°F, 170°C. Mix in flour, salt, egg, marmalade into the fruit mixture. Spoon into 2lb loaf tin which has been lined with parchment paper and bake for 1 Ω hours until well risen and firm to touch. Put cherries and chopped nuts on top. Leave to cool in tin for at least 30 mins.
Tip: To make 4, 2 lb loaf tins at once in the oven, multiply the recipe by three (e.g. 3 packets of fruit, 1 and a half pounds of fruit etc) and divide mixture between 4 loaf tins.

 *Handy Hints*

*If you're fed up with odours from your kitchen swing bin, put a handful of cat litter in the bottom of the empty bag first. It will keep the bin smelling fresh.*

*For ink and biro stains, don't bother buying an expensive stain remover. Hairspray does the same job just as well. It even works on stains that have been through the wash.*

# *Preserves*

◆◆◆◆◆◆◆◆◆◆◆◆◆◆◆◆◆◆◆◆◆◆◆◆◆◆◆◆

# PREPARATION OF FRUIT FOR JAM MAKING

1) Look over the fruit carefully – discard any bruised or damaged portions. With large fruit you need only cut away the spoilt part – with soft fruit discard the whole fruit.

2) Unless you have picked the fruit from your own garden after a spell of very fine weather, so you are certain that the fruit is very clean; it is wise to wash it. The best way to do this is to lay the fruit on fine sieves and gently pour water over it. If you actually immerse the fruit in water, it absorbs too much and will, in consequence, make you jam watery.

3) With soft fruits, transfer onto absorbent kitchen paper to dry.

4) With firm hard fruits, dry with a cloth.

5) You will notice that a lot of stress has been laid in the various recipes on stirring the sugar until dissolved. This is very important because the undissolved sugar could burn on the bottom of the pan or give you a slightly crystallised effect in the finished jam. You can always tell if the sugar is undissolved if you tap the bottom of the pan with a wooden spoon. There is a faint 'crunch' if there are any grains of sugar left.

6) A knob of butter put in while making helps to prevent scum forming. There is nothing harmful in this, but if you are entering jam for a competition it could spoil the clarity of the preserve

7) It is important to test jam as you can over boil jam and it does not set because of this. If this happens the only remedy is to mix it in with other well-made jam.

8) Stew the fruit slowly as it extracts pectin (natural setting substance), softens skin and helps jam to keep a good colour.

9) Stir until sugar has dissolved, to make certain the jam does not burn or crystallise during cooking.

10) Test early for setting. Some jams are ready within 3-5 mins, others take 10-25 mins.

11) Put a little jam on an old saucer and allow to become quite cold, then see if it forms a skin and wrinkles when pushed with a spoon or finger. Take pan off heat while waiting for jam to cool.

## APPLE LEMON JAM

2lb cooking apples (after peeling and coring)
½ pint of water
grated rind and juice of 2 lemons
2lb sugar

Simmer the apples with the water and grated rind of the lemons. When quite soft add lemon juice and sugar. Stir until the sugar has dissolved. Boil rapidly until set. Approx. cooking time 30 min.


## BLACKBERRY JAM

2lb blackberries
sugar
juice of 1 lemon

Simmer fruit and lemon juice. Sieve to remove pips. Allow 1lb sugar to each pint pulp. Reheat fruit. Stir in sugar until dissolved and boil until set. Approx. cooking time 25 mins.


## BLACKBERRY AND APPLE JAM

1lb cooking apples (after peeling and coring)
1/8 pint water
1lb blackberries
2lb sugar

Put the sliced apples and water into the preserving pan. Cook gently until the apples become soft. Add the blackberries. Continue cooking until all the fruit is soft. Stir in the sugar. Continue stirring until sugar is dissolved. Boil rapidly until jam has set. Approx. cooking time 25-30 mins.


## THE SECRET OF TENDER BLACKCURRANTS IN JAM

Simmer the fruit very gently and never add sugar until you are certain the fruit is tender. After cooking gently for about 15-20 mins try one or two currants. The skin should be so soft you can nearly 'rub it away' with your fingers.

# BLACKCURRANT JAM

1lb blackcurrants
1¼ lb sugar
¾ pint water

Put the fruit and water into preserving pan.
Simmer very slowly until the blackcurrants
are quite soft. Stir in the sugar. Boil rapidly
until set. Approx. cooking time 40 mins.

# DAMSON JAM

1/8 pint water (If fruit is ripe)
1lb damsons
1lb sugar
OR if fruit is under ripe use the
following quantities
1lb damsons
1¼ sugar
½ pint of water

Put the fruit and water into a preserving pan.
Simmer until soft, removing as many stones
as possible. Add sugar and stir until
dissolved. Boil rapidly until set. Approx.
cooking time 25-30 mins.

# GOOSEBERRY JAM

1lb gooseberries
1lb sugar
1/8 pint of water

Put the fruit and water into a preserving pan.
Simmer until soft. Add the sugar and stir until
dissolved. Boil rapidly until set. Approx
cooking time 25-30 mins

# VICTORIA PLUM CONSERVE

1lb sugar
1lb victoria plums (stoned)
1/8 pint of water

Boil the sugar and water together, stirring well
until the sugar has dissolved. Put in the
halved Victoria plums. Cook steadily until the
jam sets. Add some of the kernels from the
stones. Approx. cooking time 15 mins.

# RHUBARB JAM

1lb rhubarb
1lb sugar

Simmer the rhubarb with no water until soft. If the rhubarb is very hard, you may need 1 tablespoon of water. Stir in the sugar and lemon juice, and stir until sugar is dissolved. Boil rapidly until set. Approx. cooking time 25 mins.

# RHUBARB AND GINGER JAM

1lb rhubarb, chopped
1lb sugar
1 teaspoon powdered ginger, or
1-2 oz. crystallised ginger
juice of 1 lemon

Use the recipe for rhubarb jam. The ginger should be chopped finely. If using powdered ginger it should be sprinkled over the rhubarb. Approx cooking time 25 mins

---

# USING A JELLY BAG

*Tie the pieces of tape on the 4 'legs' of an upturned chair with a bowl underneath so that the fruit can be put into the bag and allowed to drip through gently.*

---

# APPLE JELLY

Cooking apples (unpeeled)
1 pint of water to each 2lb fruit
Sugar

Simmer the fruit until a pulp; there is no need to either peel or core the fruit. Put the pulp through a jelly bag. Leave to strain overnight. Measure the juice. Allow 1lb of sugar to each pint of juice. Stir in the sugar. Boil rapidly until set. Approx. cooking time 25-30 mins.

# APPLE AND ORANGE JELLY

2 oranges
½ pint of water
1lb cooking apples (unpeeled)
sugar

Squeeze juice from oranges and pare of rind. Chop up apples, but do not peel or core. Put apples, orange rind and water into pan. Simmer until soft. Place the fruit in a jelly bag and leave to strain. Add orange juice. Measure, and to each pint of liquid add 1lb sugar, stir until dissolved. Boil rapidly until set. Approx. cooking time 25-30 mins.

# BLACKBERRY OR BRAMBLE JELLY

1lb blackberries
1/8 pint of water
1 medium sized cooking apple
sugar

Put blackberries, water and apple into a pan. Simmer until soft. Strain the pulp through a jelly bag. Measure juice and allow 1lb sugar to each pint. Stir in sugar and continue stirring until dissolved. Boil rapidly until set. Approx. cooking time 25-30 mins.

## DIABETIC JAM (using gelatine)

1lb fruit
1 tablespoon hot water
8-10 saccharine tablets
½ oz. powdered gelatine
little water*
*Use 1/8 pint of water with soft fruit
¼ pint with firm fruit

Simmer fruit with water until soft. Crush saccharine tablets dissolved in the tablespoon of hot water. Add to the hot but not boiling fruit. Add the gelatine dissolved in the 1.8 pint of hot water. Stir briskly for several minutes. Put into small jars with firmly fitting tops and seal down. Stand in cool place. This will keep for some days. Approx. cooking time 8-15 mins.

# APPLE CHUTNEY

1lb onions (grated or finely chopped)
1 teaspoon pickling spice
½ pint of vinegar
1 teaspoon salt
2 lb apples (after peeling and coring)
1 teaspoon ground ginger
2-4 oz. dried fruit
12 oz. sugar

Put the onion into a saucepan with 1/8 pint of vinegar and simmer until nearly soft. Add the chopped apples, dried fruit, spices (tied securely in a muslin bag), salt, ground ginger and just enough vinegar to stop the mixture from burning. Cook gently until the fruit is soft, stirring from time to time. Add remainder of the vinegar and thoroughly stir in the sugar. Boil steadily until the chutney is thick. Remove pickling spices. Pour into hot jars.

# PICKLED BEETROOT

Cut the cooked beetroot into slices or cubes as desired. Put into boiling salted water (1 tablespoon salt to 1 pint water). Simmer gently for about 10 mins being careful not to break slices. Drain and pack into jars. Cover with hot spiced vinegar, i.e. white malt or ordinary malt vinegar boiled with pickling spices. Use 1 tablespoon pickling spices to each pint vinegar. Seal down at once. Store in a cool dark place.

# Fillings & Icings

••••••••••••

# BUTTERCREAM

4 oz. butter
3 oz. icing sugar

Cream the butter and sieved icing sugar until light and creamy. Flavour and colour to taste.


# DATE FILLING

1lb dates
6 oz. brown sugar
1 tablespoon lemon juice
1 oz. butter
½ pt water

Wash, stone and chop dates. Add lemon juice, sugar, butter and water. Simmer stirring constantly for 10 mins or until mixture forms a thick paste. Cool before using.


# LEMON ICING

1 egg white
8 oz. icing sugar
2 teaspoon lemon juice

Beat the egg white until frothy and sprinkle with the lemon juice. Gradually beat in the icing sugar and continue beating until mixture is smooth and thick.


# COFFEE ICING

3 oz. butter
3 tablespoons strong coffee
8 oz. icing sugar
1 teaspoon vanilla
pinch salt

Beat butter until soft; gradually add the icing sugar, salt and coffee. Beat for two mins., then add the vanilla. Let it stand for 5 mins and beat again before spreading.


# WELSH BACON SPREAD

8 oz. bacon chopped
5 tablespoons onion, grated
2 tablespoon chopped parsley
4 oz. butter
pepper to taste

Mince the bacon; mix with onion, parsley, butter and pepper. Beat well until smooth. Press into a dish and chill. Spread on toast or in a sandwich.

# MOCK CRAB SANDWICH FILLING

3 oz. marg.
1 medium onion
4 tomatoes
3 eggs
salt and pepper

Melt marg., add finely chopped onions, and simmer for 15-20 mins. Add peeled tomatoes, drop in the eggs and stir all very quickly until well mixed. Season to taste and allow to simmer, until thoroughly cooked. Sufficient for 2 loaves..


# CRANBERRY AND ORANGE SAUCE

Juice of 2 oranges
8 oz. sugar
1 lb. cranberries.

Put the orange juice and sugar into a saucepan. Allow the sugar to dissolve over a gentle heat. Add the cranberries and simmer very slowly until just tender. Serve cold.

## BIBLE CAKE

½ lb 1ˢᵗ Samuel ch 30 v 12
½ lb Judges ch 5 v 25
½ lb Jeremiah ch 6 v 20
1 lb Kings ch 4 v 22
½ lb Nahum ch 3 v 12, chopped
1 tablespoon 1ˢᵗ Samuel ch 14 v 5
3 oz. Jeremiah ch 17 v 11
2 oz. Numbers ch 17 v 8, chopped
3 tablespoons Judges ch 4 v 19
1 teaspoon Amos ch 4 v 5
1 pinch Leviticus ch 2 v 13
Season to taste with 2ⁿᵈ Chronicles ch 9 v 9.  Follow your own fruitcake recipe and bake in a moderate oven.


## BRIDES PIE

One cup of Confidence
One cup of Love
In a pan of Happiness
Mix the above
Add a pinch of Tenderness, a tablespoon of Twist
Stir well in the Sunshine
Roll out the Loving Crust
Flour with Contentment,
Keep free from Strife
Fill with Understanding
Bake well for Life.

# Conversion Tables

## TEMPERATURE

| | | |
|---|---|---|
| 240°C | 475°F | regulo 9 |
| 230°C | 450°F | regulo 8 |
| 220°C | 425°F | regulo 7 |
| 200°C | 400°F | regulo 6 |
| 190°C | 375°F | regulo 5 |
| 180°C | 350°F | regulo 4 |
| 160°C | 325°F | regulo 3 |
| 150°C | 300°F | regulo 2 |
| 140°C | 275°F | regulo 1 |
| 120°C | 250°F | regulo ½ |
| 110°C | 225°F | regulo ¼ |

## VOLUME

| | |
|---|---|
| 3.4 l | 6 pints |
| 2.75 l | 5 pints |
| 2.25 l | 4 pints |
| 1.7 l | 3 pints |
| 1.4 l | 2½ pints |
| 850 ml | 1½ pints |
| 570 ml | 1 pint |
| 425 ml | ¾ pint |
| 380 ml | ⅔ pint |
| 280 ml | ½ pint |
| 200 ml | 7 fl oz |
| 170 ml | 6 fl oz |
| 140 ml | ¼ pint / 5 fl oz |
| 115 ml | 4 fl oz |
| 70 ml | ⅛ pint |

## WEIGHT

| | |
|---|---|
| 1.35 kg | 3 lb |
| 900 g | 2 lb |
| 680 g | 1½ lb |
| 450 g | 1 lb |
| 400 g | 14 oz |
| 340 g | 12 oz |
| 285 g | 10 oz |
| 225 g | 8 oz |
| 200 g | 7 oz |
| 170 g | 6 oz |
| 140 g | 5 oz |
| 115 g | 4 oz |
| 85 g | 3 oz |
| 70 g | 2½ oz |
| 55 g | 2 oz |
| 45 g | 1½ oz |
| 30 g | 1 oz |
| 15 g | ½ oz |